Playing on Your Last String

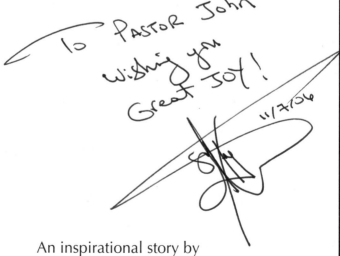

To Pastor John
Wishing you
Great Joy!

11/7/06

An inspirational story by

DR. RAP

Cataloging Data

Dr. Rap (Kojoglanian, Samuel A., MS, MD)
        Playing on Your Last String / Samuel A. Kojoglanian, MS, MD
(Dr. Rap).
        224p.
        ISBN 0-9706625-0-5
        1. Achievement motivation in adolescence.   2. Attitude
(Psychology)   3. Goal-directed behavior.   4. Values in adolescence.
I. Title   II. Author: Kojoglanian, Samuel A., MS, MD   II. Author:
Dr. Rap
        158.1   LC:

Published by AV Records
Printed in the United States of America

Dedicated to

MOM & DAD

YOU HAVE MADE
THE DREAM POSSIBLE

About The Author

Samuel A. Kojoglanian (Kojo – glan – yan), MS, MD, aka Dr. Rap, is a Board Certified Internist and Cardiologist.

He received his Bachelors in Psychobiology from the University of Southern California (USC), Masters of Science in Anatomy and Medical Doctor degree from USC School of Medicine (now known as Keck School of Medicine of the University of Southern California).

He completed his Internal Medicine Residency at Huntington Memorial Hospital in Pasadena, CA.

He completed his fellowship in Cardiology at Kaiser Permanente Los Angeles Medical Center, becoming an interventional cardiologist.

Dr. Kojoglanian is also known as Dr. Rap. After witnessing tragic trauma involving youth and their families in Southern California emergency rooms, Dr. Rap was inspired to intercept the violence and prevent it by incorporating his anti-violence and anti-drug message into rap form. His first CD entitled *Licensed to Heal* was released in 1996. A second CD entitled *Cut to the Heart* was recently released on his record label, AV Records.

By visiting schools, prisons and youth events, Dr. Rap aspires to touch the hearts of a broken generation and challenge this generation to greatness.

Dr. Kojoglanian resides in Southern California; enjoys jogging, playing the sax, golf, and basketball; collects model lighthouses; and loves to visit the ocean-side.

Acknowledgments

I thank the following people who have impacted my life greatly:

Uncle Pete and Aunt Zella for loving us when we came to America.

Mrs. Hixson (Davis), my 8th grade Civics teacher at Tyner Jr. High School, who challenged me to become a leader.

Mr. O'Neal, my 10th grade English teacher at McCallie High School, who worked to strengthen my weaknesses.

Special thanks to:

Vicken Aharonian, MD; Agop Aintablian, MD; Althea Alexander; Pastor John Andrus; Martin Bobrowsky, MD; Jeff Bruss, MD; Pastor Koko Garabedian; Sako Garabedian; Shahe Garabedian; Jaime Garcia, MD; Mike Jorgensen, MD; Garbis Kahkejian; Martin Laichtman, MD; Chris Mangum; Prakash Mansukhani, MD; Samuel Marchese; Vatche Mekhjian; Mgo Pambakian; Fernando Roth, MD; Pastors Jim and Melinda Scott; Milton Smith, MD; Don Sprenger; Pastor Bobby Thomas; Charlotte Young; and Robert and Denise Zeilstra, who have supported, encouraged and inspired me.

My patients, who give me the privilege to share in their lives.

My indispensable cath lab crew.

Huntington Memorial Hospital, for backing the birth of Dr. Rap.

Kaiser Permanente at Los Angeles for providing me with the opportunity to train in Cardiology.

Lynn Lanning, editor and typesetter, who masterfully tackled this project and went beyond the 2nd mile to insure its success.

Arthur Bahadourian who selflessly gave of his time and energy to create the cover design of this book.

Johnny Hart (*The Wizard of Id*), Hank Ketcham (*Dennis the Menace*), and Steve Moore (*In the Bleachers*) for their gracious permission to use their cartoon strips.

Andy, Houry, Armen and Raffi Khechoumian, for your love.

Arpy, my sister, for inspiring me to listen to the hearts of people.

God my Savior, for His undeserved Grace.

Before You Begin

This book is written for anyone with a dream. Whether that dream is alive and burning with passion within the chambers of your heart, or is dead, buried in the drudge of fear and regrets, this book is for you.

This book is written for the mom who is changing diapers between two toddlers, and somehow courageously manages to work.

For the dad, busy paying Uncle Sam.

For the young lady, aspiring to become a doctor.

For the young man, aspiring to get into graduate school.

For the one who wants to be a fireman, astronaut, an artist, a dancer, teacher, singer, sports star, or professional.

For the one who has so many things to do, and so little time.

This book is for you who have failed and are failing.

For you who have succeeded and conquered success.

For you who don't know where to begin.

For you who are leading the pack.

And for you who are lost in the pack.

Playing on Your Last String will challenge you

> to come out of your comfort zone, place a mantle of discipline around you and take action.

It will encourage you

> to march beyond your failures.

It will inspire you

> to dream again and soar above your limitations.

It will teach you

> to live life at the moment and to its fullest.

It will guide you

> to reach your destined hopes.

There are practical steps in this book that systematically will help you attain your dreams. It has warning signs to caution you and stories to cheer you. Every section ends with "Take 5 with Dr. Rap," a short time out to reflect on the essentials. This book will provide you with strength for today and hope for tomorrow.

Enjoy!

Contents

Section 1

Purpose

*If you don't stand for something,
you'll fall for anything.*

—Author unknown

Blond & Blue

"Hey boy."
"Where'd you come from?"
 It was a group.
 All blond.
 Blue eyed.
 Pointing fingers and laughing.
"You a foreigner or something boy?"
"Where'd you get them clothes?"
"My dogs wouldn't wear those!"
"Don't he speak?"
"Maybe he's dumb or something."
"You dumb boy, huh, you dumb?"
 They busted out in laughter, like old rusty instruments out of tune
 and out of synch.
"Ask him if he wants to play."
 They tossed the football over to me.
"Well boy, you wanna play?"
 I picked the football off the lawn and stared at this oddly shaped toy.
 I'd come from the Armenian quarters in Jerusalem, where I was born.
 There, I'd played with a round ball.
 I stared curiously at the football as my audience carefully examined
 me as if I were an insignificant specimen under their giant
 microscope.
 And then.
 To their fondest delight.
 I tried to dribble the football.
 They were on the grass.
 Rolling.
 Laughing.
 To the point of tears.

I shrugged my shoulders and started to pull back.
I was only nine.
My new home was a place called "America."
What an odd place I thought to myself.
People roll on the ground.
And they've got funny looking toys.

Paganini's String

It was a packed house.
And the great violinist, Niccolò Paganini graced the stage.
Surrounded by a full orchestra, he filled the arena with majestic music.
While performing a favorite violin concerto in front of a mesmerized Italian audience, he helplessly witnessed one of his violin strings snap as it sluggishly dangled down his instrument.
Puzzled, but relying on his genius, this great violinist improvised, playing on the three strings.
But to his surprise as well as the conductor's, a second string snapped.
The crowd gazed in utter suspense.
The conductor fearfully focused on the two strings, and forced his hand to move the baton.
Paganini's heart raced as his fingers skillfully mastered the two remaining strings.
As the end of the piece was nearing, the unthinkable took place: the third string snapped.
Three strings dangled from his instrument as if to mock Paganini.
Paganini and one string.
Paganini kept playing with all his heart and might while his bow elegantly danced on one string.
The soothing sound of the remaining string gently forced its way into the hearts of the audience, who now was caught in the delightful web of shock.
The melody from one string majestically ascended above every note played that night.
Paganini and one string.
The last baton stroke found its way.

The last notes reached the ears.
The last string stood its ground.
The orchestra froze in awe.
And the audience jolted to its feet and cheered incessantly.
Paganini and one string.
Taking the hits.
Standing firm.
Tenaciously determined.
Whole-heartedly believing.
Possessed with uncompromising passion.
Empowered by unmistakable purpose.
And fueled by unquenchable desire.
Paganini.
With a mission.
Paganini.
With a vision.
Paganini.
Playing on his last string.

-3-

Your Own Calcutta

A certain young boy wanted to know how he could make a difference in people's lives.
He wanted to learn.
He wanted to give.
He wanted to be heard.
Having read about Mother Teresa, he decided to write her a letter, asking her how he could impact people as she had in her own world.
Many months passed.
He didn't hear from her.
"She didn't get the letter... or maybe she didn't want to answer," he thought.
Then one day, the young boy's mother handed him a letter.
Addressed to him.
From Calcutta, India.
He frantically ripped the envelope and read four words.
Four words that dripped with purpose and passion.
Four words that tunneled their way through his heart.
Four words that glistened with life.
Four words that danced with promise.
Four words that changed the course of his life.
Simple but deep words of advice:

"Find your own Calcutta."
—Mother Teresa

-4-

Soul Play

My friend tells me that when doctors were searching through the wreckage and crushed bodies in the maternity ward, they found baby Nareh, crying for refuge.

Like Moses in the Nile River, floating safely into the gentle arms of Pharaoh's daughter, so too Nareh found her way to safety in the aftershocks, two months after the Armenian earthquake of 1988.

Why was her life spared when many died?

How could the concrete crumple in such a way as to not crush her?

How could the glass gash in such a way as to not cut her?

How could the rattle of the earth ricochet in such a way as to not destroy her?

By the age of three, Nareh would be composing songs on the piano.

By the age of eleven, Nareh would be winning in international competitions.

She practices endlessly every day, but doesn't have a piano in her apartment because she doesn't want to disturb her neighbors.

Now at twelve, Nareh Arghamanyan is on her way to finding world recognition.

At the age of nine, she was on a concert tour.

Sold out as soon as the tickets went on sale.

Nareh had a high fever and felt ill.

Mom was by her side.

"Nareh, sweetheart, I don't want you to play. You are much too sick. We will re-schedule for these nice people."

She held her and felt tremendous heat radiate through her daughter's body.

"You cannot play, dear."

"Mom..."

"No, you will not play... your body is too weak."

"But mom... "

Nareh desperately begged her mom to let her play.

But her mother stood her ground, "No Nareh, we need to see the doctor. Your body is too weak."

"But mom... I don't play with my body... I play with my soul!"

That nine-year old girl stepped on stage.

And to the delight of her audience... played with soul!

-5-

The "Promise" Land

My family left our homeland when I was nine years old.
Jerusalem, Israel became Chattanooga, Tennessee.
David Street became Merry Wood Lane.
My Armenian heritage transformed into baseball and apple pies.
Stuffed Squash became hamburgers and French fries (Double-Double at In-N-Out... yum).
Soccer turned into football.
Sandals became Nikes.
Pantaloons became Levi's.
Walking to school became riding on a yellow bus, with a funny sidearm that flashed and read, "STOP."
The market place with fresh fish and foods became grocery stores with cans, plastics, and fruit tainted with insecticide.
Bargaining in small stores turned into paying the full price at the mall.
The Mediterranean Sea became chlorinated pools.
Family dinners on rooftops under beautiful stars became a kitchen with fluorescent lights.
Five learned languages dwindled into two.
Six days of school turned into five.
Bethlehem, the birthplace of Jesus, "King of the Jews" was compared to Graceland, where Elvis the king of rock and roll was buried.
Hard core discipline in schools turned into recess.
Familiarity turned into the unknown.
Simplicity turned into the complex.
Teamwork turned into individualism.

And there I was.
A boy of nine.
In the Land of the Free.
Where my parents brought me.
They brought their family with a goal, a purpose and a dream.
My parents worked fifteen hours a day in Jerusalem for years.
As a child, I never understood my parents' workload.
Was it to pursue power?
Was it to pursue riches?
Was it to get even?
Was it to survive?
When they moved, they left behind their friends.
Their luxury.
Their land.
Their shop.
Their leisure.
Their all.
For their kids.
And as I grew older, I didn't have to look to the football stadiums,
basketball arenas, baseball fields or concert halls to find my heroes.
My heroes were in my own house.
For they had sacrificed everything so their children could grow up
in what they called the "Promise" Land.

-6-

Silver on Ice

Pursuing a dream requires intense effort.
It is 1998.
Nagano, Japan.
Winter Olympics.
The female ice skaters are battling for the gold.
Michelle Kwan graces the ice with poise, and shines.
At the end of it all.
Years of unwavering practice.
Years of sweat.
Years of harsh training.
And years of relentless competition.
She's awarded the silver.
Reporters are in her face.
Jamming mics to her lips.
Some of them have no sense of privacy and don't know their limits.
"So, how does it feel to lose the gold?" they ask bluntly.
"I didn't lose the gold," Kwan kindly states.
"I won the silver!"
To win, one must have the desire.
No purpose defines a life that's worthless.
Ever since her quest began, Kwan has clinched four world titles.
She skates.
She sweats.
She works.
She dreams.
And in the next winter Olympics, look for Kwan to capture it all.

-7-

Brains on Ice

To some, it's the ice rink.
To others, it's ice.
Let me explain.
I took care of a 16 year-old teen in the Intensive Care Unit as a
senior resident at Huntington Memorial Hospital.
He was alive, and yet dead.
He was awake, and yet unaware.
He was breathing, and yet without breath.
He was existing, and yet not present.
His name is not important.
But what he did is.
He was an intelligent, joyful, courageous son.
He was a young, caring, and fun loving brother.
He was a courteous, helpful, and loyal friend.
One night.
Hanging out with his friends.
He got hold of ice.
Not talking about ice as in frozen water.
We're talking ice as in crystal methamphetamine, an illicit drug.
Whether he smoked it or injected it, I don't know.
The form of use doesn't matter.
What it did to him does.
In a matter of minutes his friends said that he was "trippn' out and
losing it."
He crashed to the floor.
No one seemed to care.
But his friends began to freak when he started to convulse and
foam at the mouth.
911 was called.

Music turned into sirens.
Laughter turned into tears.
Party turned into sorrow.
He was rushed to the emergency room on the night when I was
on call.
Tubes were jammed in his face.
IV's[1] pierced his non-scarred skin.
And he lay there with open eyes.
An MRI[2] of his brain revealed that a major portion of his brain was
infarcted.[3]

Though he lay awake, he would never speak again.
Never to be aware of his environment.
Never to understand a spoken word.
Never to experience love.
Never to smile.
And never to laugh.
It takes a lot of courage to live life.
But drugs didn't give him courage.
Drugs stripped him cold.
And ripped his life.

---

[1] *IV's* (pronounced "Eye-Vee's"): Intravenous; tubes inserted into the veins to allow
 medications and fluids to go directly into the blood stream.
[2] *MRI* (Magnetic Resonance Imagery): machine that images soft tissue, bone, and blood vessels.
[3] *infarcted:* turned to dead tissue because of a sudden cutting off of the arterial blood supply.

His prognosis was tragic.
His family was shattered.
His father was broken.
His mother was crushed.
His brother was shocked.
He was only 16.
Ready to conquer.
Ready to live.
Ready to soar.
Ready to give.
But he would not... because he could not.
His father cried, "Doc, he's got no hope, does he?"
I held his hand and looked into his eyes without saying a word.
He understood.
One crack at the world of drugs sent this young man to the land of ventilators, silence, despair, darkness and doom.
One crack at the world of drugs sent this man's family to the land of tears, loss and sorrow.
One crack.
One try.
One laugh.
One party.
One sniff.
One time.
One second.
One move.
One life.
One death.

-8-

Yellow Taxis

Few people have convictions and a purpose as Sanjeev.
Sanjeev was an Indian immigrant.
While walking the streets of Manhattan, New York with his American friend John, Sanjeev said, "I hear cricket."
"What? Man you're crazy," John exclaimed, "How can you hear a cricket. We got the taxis, horns, buses, people... thousands of people... man this is New York... and you hear a cricket?"
"Yes, I hear cricket."
"OK Sanjeev, where's your little cricket friend hanging out?"
Sanjeev closed his eyes.
People were rushing.
Businessmen were pushing.
Faces were cold, reflecting desperate hopes, unfulfilled dreams, unmet goals with an unknown future.
Gazes were set straight ahead.
Purses were held tightly.
No time to speak.
No time to chatter.
No time for others.
No time for themselves.
They were running.
Running faster.
Running harder.
Run.
Go.
Go faster.
To get somewhere.
To get something.
To be someone.
Sanjeev opened his eyes.

Turned his body 180 degrees and started walking towards a planted
tree about three feet away.
He started digging around the soil.
Looked up at John with a victorious smile.
And said, "Here is my friend, the cricket."
"Man Sanjeev, how in the world did you hear this thing… is this like
a religious thing?"
"Religious? You are crazy John boy," Sanjeev replied. "Listen to me."
Sanjeev took out the pennies from his pocket.
"I am only to do this one time. You listen."
John looked on, shaking his head in disbelief.
Sanjeev held the pennies in his palm.
And then, to John's amazement, Sanjeev threw them on the
pavement.
In an instant second.
Without delay.
And without doubt.
Every head within half a block turned to the sound of coins
showering the streets of Manhattan.
"See John boy."
"You see the people."
"They all of them turn around."

It depends what we are listening for.
I wonder what we would have heard.
So let me ask you.
What do you hear?
Where do you stand?
Would you have heard the cricket?
You and I would have marched right past it.
After all, we have to get somewhere!
Run.
Run faster.
Run harder.

Shouldn't snooze.
We might lose.
We might miss out.
Frantically, in doubt.
Did you know that humans are the only species that run faster
when they are lost?

On the other hand, there are the coins.
I would have glanced.
I would have noticed.
So where do we stand?
This is not a lecture.
It's face to face.
Eye to eye.
Heart to heart.
Regarding questions that will one day confront you and me.
So stop running.
Stop running so fast.
Stop running so fast that you forget yourself and your loved ones
around you.
And answer these questions.
Do you have a purpose?
Do you have four strings, or are you playing on one?
What do you want out of life?
What purpose does your life hold when all is said and done?

Is it to pay the bills?
Is it just to make it through another day?
Another week?
Till you get your next pay?
Is it to attain power?
Is it to move on up?
Is it to get that position or possession?
Or is it to be on top?
Is it a diploma?
Is it an office with a view?
Is it for others?
Or is it for you?
Is it with joy?
Or is it with dread?
Is it for revenge?
Or is it because of something somebody said?
You know why you exist?
You know what you're doing?
You know who you are?
You know where you're going?

Whatever it is.
Stop.
Slow down.
Reflect.
Define your purpose.
And remember.
Whatever your purpose, your entire life not only revolves around it,
but it defines your very existence.

-9-

Beyond the Track

In the early 1900s a young black child grew up in Cleveland, in a home which he described as "materially poor but spiritually rich." Charlie Paddock, a famous athlete visited this child's school and spoke to the student body.

At that time, Paddock was considered the fastest human being alive. The children were mesmerized by his presence.

The fastest man in the world had set foot in their small world.

As the little black child starred at Paddock, his eyes focused intently but his mind transferred him on the track field.

Paddock said, "Listen! What do you want to be? You name it and then believe that God will help you be it."

That day, the little black child decided that he wanted to become the fastest human being on earth.

The boy ran with unfailing determination to the track coach and shared with him of his newly found dream.

His coach smiled and said, "It's great to have a dream, but to attain your dream you must build a ladder to it. Sit down son. Sit down and listen to me. Here is the ladder to your dreams. The first rung is determination! You have that, son; I see it in you. The second rung is dedication! I know you have the desire, son, I see it in your eyes. The third rung is discipline! We will work on this one, son. Yes, we got some work to do on you. And the fourth is attitude! Attitude will pull you across the finish line every time, son. Attitude will shape your life, son."

The little black child ran with passion.
Dreams turned into determination.
Determination turned into dedication.
Dedication turned into discipline.
Days turned into months.
Months turned into years.
And attitude turned into a well deserved spot in the Olympics.
The 1936 Berlin Olympics.
The child was now a man.
And this man returned home with medals.
Four gold medals.
He won the 100 meter dash and broke the Olympic and
world records for the 200 meter.
His broad jump record lasted for twenty-four years.
His name?
A man with boyhood dreams.
A man of purpose and destiny.
A man of desire and attitude.
Was no other than Jesse Owens.

-10-

The Zode

Did I ever tell you about the young Zode?
Who came to two signs at the fork in the road?
One said to Place One, and the other, Place Two.
So the Zode had to make up his mind what to do.
Well… the Zode scratched his head, and his chin and his pants.
And he said to himself, "I'll be taking a chance.
If I go to Place One. Now, that place may be hot!
And so, how do I know if I'll like it or not?
On the other hand though, I'll be sort of a fool
If I go to Place Two and find it too cool.
In that case I may catch a terrible earache and die!
So Place Two may be best! On the other hand though…
What might happen to me if Place Two is too low?
I might get some very strange pain in my toe!
So Place One may be best," and he started to go.
Then he stopped, and he said, "On the other hand though…
On the other hand… other hand… other hand though… "
And for 36 hours and a half that poor Zode
Made starts and made stops at the fork in the road.
Saying, "Don't take a chance. No! You may not be right."
Then he got an idea that was wonderfully bright!
"Play safe!" cried the Zode. "I'll play safe. I'm no dunce!
I'll simply start out for both places at once!"
And that's how the Zode who would not take a chance
Got no place at all with a split in his pants.
    —Theodor Geisel (Dr. Seuss)

"The Zode," aka "Ode to the Zode," by Theodor Geisel (Dr. Seuss);
  unpublished manuscript. This printing is authorized by Dr. Seuss Enterprises.

DENNIS THE MENACE

"HOW COME EVERYONE WANTS TO BE WHERE THEY AREN'T?"

Take 5 with Dr. Rap

Once upon a time there were four people named Everybody, Somebody, Nobody and Anybody.

When there was an important job to be done, Everybody was sure that Somebody would do it.

Anybody could have done it.

But Nobody did.

When Nobody did it, Everybody got angry because it was Anybody's job.

Everybody thought that Somebody would do it.

But Nobody realized that Anybody wouldn't do it.

So it ended up that Everybody blamed Somebody when Nobody did what Anybody could have done in the first place.

—Author Unknown

Don't zip to the next page.

Don't just be anybody… be somebody that does something with a great purpose.

If you didn't answer this before, answer it now.

What's your purpose in life?

Where'd you come from?

Where are you at?

And where are you going?

In fact, why are you going where you're going?

To give you an example, I'd like to share with you Kaiser Los Angeles Medical Center's motto:

Mission:
People are our foundation.
Quality is our credo.
Service is our culture.
Access is our opportunity.

Vision:
To be a high performing member-focused healthcare delivery system dedicated to improving the health and well being of the communities it serves in a time of significant change.

… Serving people with great quality to better the community today and in the future…

A great motto!

Take it from me. No matter what, **you** have a purpose in life.
Seek it.
Find it.
Cherish it.
And share it.

Whether it's a simple word or a short sentence, write your purpose down and pursue it with passion. There is something about etching your mission on paper… you somehow bring it to life. But remember, if drugs are in the picture, your purpose is dead, no matter what you believe, and no matter how zealous you are.

My purpose:

Signature:

Date:

Section II

Plan and Preparation

Great things are not done by impulse,
but by a series of small things
that are brought together.

—Vincent Van Gogh

Snap Shot

Before you start.
Take a snap shot.
Where are you going?
How are you gonna get there?
What are you aiming for?
What are you aiming at?
If you're aimless, you'll be a hundred percent accurate... because you never took aim.
You never shot.
You never dreamt.
You never aspired.
But if you have a dream.
A goal.
An aspiration.
You have begun your journey.
It's work.
Sweat.
Hardship.
Rejections.
Failures.
Surprises.
Successes.
And because of your dreams today, you have begun to create your tomorrows.

~12~

Dr. J's Kitchen Chairs

I'll never forget the first time I witnessed Dr. J (Julius Erving) slam-dunk.
I knew it then.
That when I grew up.
I'd be playing in the NBA like Dr. J.
And no time was wasted.
I got my parents to buy me a new NBA backboard.
I'd wake up early in the mornings.
Get the kitchen chairs.
And place them on the driveway.
Mom wasn't happy about her chairs, but she let me anyway.
Some say I was spoiled.
I just say, "I'm loved."
I'd space the chairs about five feet apart from each other and weave through them, dribbling the ball as fast as I could. I'd move swiftly, and flying by my last opponent, I would glide in the air... Sam Julius Erving Kojoglanian... with only one second left on the clock... and to the dismay of my opponents... score the last shot. My teammates would be going absolutely mad.
The crowd would be rocking the arena. And I would be the hero.
And then back to the chairs.
The chairs were the tenacious defensive players.
I'd arrange them again.
I'd mark the half court line.
And take the shots.

Five.

Four.

Three.

Two.

One.

He shoots.

And… let's do this again.

That one didn't count, I'd convince myself.

Five.

Four.

Over and over again.

Until I made it.

And that would be the one that counted.

I'd ask family members to hold up a broom in their hands. They too were the defense. And I had to arch the ball in such a way to bypass the ten-foot tall defense.

I attended summer camps.

Sweat.

Run.

Hurt.

Run some more.

Come home aching.

Crash.

Then wake up early and go again.

With a goal in my mind.

To make it on the high school varsity team.

The coach had seen me.

And liked me.

He knew I worked hard.

And then it came time for the tryouts.

Weeks of grueling running.
Round and round the track.
Sun beating on my head.
Then back in the gym.
For sprints.
Until my legs would no longer listen to my stubborn demands.
Drills.
Plays.
Plans.
On the board.
In your mind.
On the floor.
Pushups.
More.
And more.
No time for wimps.
Push it.
Up and down the bleachers.
Up and down the bleachers again.
Weight room.
Bench press.
Curling iron.
Then the day.
My Dr. J day.
Where I would make the team.
I'd be a sports hero.
I knew in my heart that it would happen.
The names were called.
Six-foot-five made it.
One by one.

Name after name.
Celebrations.
Surprises.
Dreams.
Two people left on the sidelines.
They didn't make it.
They just stood there.
Embarrassed.
Rejected.
Failures.
The others glanced at the two in a victorious glare.
The two were crushed.
Beaten.
Defeated.
Demoralized.
Disheartened.
Dejected.
Distraught.
And downcast.
I know how they felt.
I know how they hurt.
Because.
One of the two.
On the sidelines.
Standing there.
Without dignity.
Without hope.
And without a spot on the varsity team.
Was me.

-13-

Brushing for Life

Mike was my best friend in junior high.
An avid golfer, he could tee off right or left-handed.
I went by his house one day and found him brushing his teeth.
Five minutes.
Ten minutes.
Half an hour.
"Mike, what's up? What in the world are you doing?"
"I've been brushing my teeth for two hours now!"
"What? Are you crazy?"
"I see the dentist on Monday. I haven't brushed my teeth in a while…
so I'm making up for it now."
Both of us busted into laughter as toothpaste soaked saliva streaked
down his chin, and glazed the newly shampooed carpet.
Both of us knew that it didn't make a difference.
If he didn't want cavities, he should have been brushing every day.
I didn't even think much of it then.
But it just hit me.
That's exactly how some of us live or would like to live our lives.
Crash course.
Quick fix.
Easy money.
Buy and sell on Ameritrade.
Don't got time to plan.
Don't want to sweat.
Don't want to work all those years.

But in case you didn't figure, most things in life don't come easy.
Like getting a diploma.
Or shooting par on a golf course.
Or having cavity free teeth.
So set your goals.
Set up your gear.
Put on your mantle.
Prepare for the droughts.
Inquire.
Load up.
Persevere.
And push ahead.
Cause we're about to play hard-ball.

IN THE BLEACHERS

By Steve Moore

"Come back! I didn't say 'dentistry'! I said 'destiny'!
Our team has a rendezvous with *destiny*!!"

~14~

No Hopes in Hoops

After the humiliating sideline scene, I was called into the coach's office.

"You know Sam, you're a hard worker."

I didn't hear anything else.

He babbled till kingdom come.

I was in my own zone.

He had crushed my dreams.

He had stripped me of my chances.

I felt as if he had publicly demeaned me by etching my spot on the sidelines.

All those mornings.

I'd wake up.

Get those kitchen chairs on the driveway.

All those hopes.

All those dreams.

Now I know what it feels like when I, as a physician, give unfortunate news to a patient or a family. They don't really hear anything else as I babble on to get a point across. Emotions set in. Their heart beats faster. Their throat becomes dry. They don't care about the medical jargon. They just want to know if they're going to be all right.

And sitting in the coach's office, I didn't hear another word.

Five minute lecture.

I wanted to scream.

I wanted to cry.

I wanted to die.

I wanted to yell for help.
I wanted someone's comforting words.
I left the room.
Crushed.
I didn't cry, but my heart sank and bled with tears.
I went home, dejected.
And Never.
Never again.
Did I place the kitchen chairs out on the driveway.

-15-

Distinction

Plan and stand.
Prepare and stand out.
Not in clothes.
Not in poles.
Not in money.
Not in personality.
Not in positions.
Not in possessions.
Not in affiliations.
Not in appearance.
Not in poetic jargons.
Not in diplomatic bargains.
Not in portfolios
Not in diplomas.
These things don't last.
They have no eternal value.

Stand out.
In service.
In justice.
In humility.
In generosity.
In mercy.
In courtesy.
In patience.
In allegiance.

In honor.
In character.
In truth.
In faith.
In kindness.
And in love.

And in so doing, touch the hearts and souls of the people you meet.
—Dr. Rap

-16-

A Father's Plan of Love

At times life takes a different course.
A turn you did not expect.
An event you could not have imagined.
A circumstance you could not avoid.
A time for which you could not plan.
Armenia has had its shares of cruel awakenings, and in 1988 it felt the harsh reality of uncertainty once again.
That year an earthquake rattled Armenia, and over 30,000 people were buried alive in a matter of seconds.
After the quake, a father frantically rushed to his son's school.
Upon his arrival, he noted that the building was completely defaced and demolished.
He had made a promise to his son years ago, "No matter what son, I will always be by your side and be there for you."
He glanced at the pile of debris and felt doom and despair attack his heart.
He knelt on his knees and began to cry, rocking back and forth to comfort himself.
What could he do?
He was too late.
But what of the promise?
What if his son were alive?
The commitment he made to his son forced him off his knees and possessed him with supernatural determination.
He had no specific plan.
Nor could he ever have prepared for this tragedy.
But his love for his son gave him the power to move.
He remembered where his son's classroom was located.
It was in the back right corner of the building.
He rushed to the spot and started digging through the rubble.

As he was digging, other terrified parents arrived on the scene, searching for their children.

All were yelling, "My son, my daughter," and beating their breasts in helpless defeat.

Some parents tried to pull this father back.

"It's too late! They're dead! You can't help! Go back home!"

To each person, he replied with tears, "I won't stop until I find my son!"

Stone by stone.

Inch by inch.

He kept clearing and continued to dig for his son as stone and glass bruised and cut his hands.

The fire chief tried to pull him back, warning him of the fires that were breaking out in nearby neighborhoods.

But this father's determination grew stronger by the minute.

The police were now on the scene and warned him that he was endangering others and should go home.

To everyone who tried to stop him, he would reply, "Please help. Please help. Please help me."

No one helped.

They just stared.

Courageously he proceeded alone.

He dug for six hours.

Which turned into 12.

A day passed.

Then 36 hours without stopping to eat or drink or sleep.

By now his hands were bleeding.

His back was arched and pounding with pain.

He did not care for food.

His love drove him in the search of his son.

In the 40th hour, he pulled back a boulder.

As he pulled back the boulder, he heard an angelic voice.
The voice of his son, Armand.
He screamed his son's name, "Armand!"
"Father! It's me, father! I told my friends not to worry. I told them
that if you were alive, you'd save me, and when you saved me,
they'd be saved. I told them, father. Because I'd knew you'd come."
There were 13 other children still alive along with Armand.
When the building collapsed during the earthquake, it had made a
wedge like a triangle, saving the lives of the children.
Armand's father yelled, "Come on out, my son!"
"No, father. Let the other kids out first. I know you'll get me! I know
you'll be there for me!"

A father and his son.
A father and his promise.
A father and his determination.
A father and his love.

Sometimes plans are put aside.
And preparation goes to naught.
Sometimes experience offers no help.
And wisdom escapes your grasp.

But love…
In life or in death…
Always.
Yes, always wins.

-17-

Little More

"Let me hear you play, Sam."
 So I started to play.
"No, no, not that part. The middle piece."
"The middle piece?"
"Yes, the middle piece."
 I positioned my fingers on the keys of my tenor sax.
 And bit on the mouthpiece in complete horror.
 I knew I was in trouble when the whole band stopped its course and
 looked at me.
 We had been practicing all week for the high school homecoming
 game.
 I had practiced all the songs.
 Except this one.
 I'd wing it.
 I thought.
 In fact, there were four sax players.
 They would cover me.
 I started to play but the notes appeared very foreign.
 And the more the band stared, the harder the notes became.
 I wanted to tell the director that I wasn't prepared to play.
 But I didn't.
 How he knew, I don't know.
 What about all the other songs?
 I knew those.
 He didn't ask me to play those.
 He asked me to play the one I didn't know.
 So I played.

I'll never forget the look on the alto saxophonist's face.
He shook his head as if he were a king.
As if he knew all the tunes in the world.
As if he pitied me.
I honestly wanted to hit him.
Pick up my sax and knock him over the head with it.
Let's see who's laughing now, you alto saxophone head...
I wanted to tell him to take his arrogant self out of my face...
But I held my big mouth.
The director saw (and heard) my misery.
"Sam, you've done great on everything... just a little more work on this one... OK?"
"OK."

Just a little more work.
A little more planning.
A little more preparing.
A little more effort.
And a little more exertion.
Just a little more... can make all the difference.

-18-

Me, Dr. J & the NBA

OK.
So before you, my plan I lay.
I wasn't meant to be Dr. J.
Maybe I wasn't meant to play.
In the NBA.
Yesterday.
Or today.
Although I did pray.
I just can't be Dr. J.
Every morning on Monday.
Tuesday.
Wednesday.
Thursday.
Friday.
And Saturday.
It was I and the kitchen chairs on display.
On the driveway.
Where dad parked his blue classic Chevrolet.
Swish, swish, swish.
I heard a gentle voice in my heart say.
"You gave all you had… don't dismay."
Replay.
"You gave all you had… don't dismay."

-19-

Failing Successfully

I remember sitting in English class one week after failing to make it on the basketball team.

We were reading short stories.

Somehow the subject of basketball came up.

My English teacher, Mr. O'Neil, had watched the basketball tryouts a week earlier.

He had seen it all.

When he said it, I wasn't embarrassed.

Just surprised.

"If you give it your all, you'll make it. It's very true. Well, I take that back. I've never seen anybody work as hard as Sam... and not make the team."

Have you ever felt like everyone in the room was staring at you?

Like when you walk into a meeting late, and several hundred inquisitive eyes track your every movement and analyze the fine details of your pensive face?

"I've never seen anybody work as hard as Sam... and not make the team."

Did he really just say that?

Was I supposed to say something?

Mr. O'Neil looked at me and asked, "Why didn't you go out for the B-Team, Sam."

"I didn't want the B-Team," I said.

"Yeah, I don't blame you," he said.

Had I given up too quickly?

Was I too picky?

You can't just get what you want when you want it.

You work.
Sweat.
And if you fail.
You try again.
And again.
Until success is yours.
But that's the problem with success.
What's it mean to me?
What's it mean to you?
Varsity teams?
Diplomas?
Possessions?
Money?
Power?
Material?
More material?
And even more material?
I had given my all.
And I knew it.
On the laps around the track.
Running up and down the bleachers.
Doing the pushups.
The drills.
The short sprints.
I was not only there.
But I was *all* there.
And I poured my very being into the practices, down to the last sweat.

I don't want to send the wrong message to the kids who read this book.

I don't want to tell them to dream, attempt, and if you fail, just quit.

People shorter than six feet tall play in the NBA.

They hustle, score and slam.

I do think I could have ultimately made the team, even if it were the B-team.

But I made a choice.

To concentrate on what meant more to me than basketball.

That was my dream to be a doctor.

I had tried basketball.

For me, the sheer attempt was a miracle.

I will never forget those kitchen chairs.

How they played defense, and never once argued.

How my mom was gracious enough to let me drag those chairs out on the driveway.

How my friends and family would hold up a broom to force me to have an arch on my shot.

I treasure those memories fondly.

For I attempted.

I tried.

And I was all there.

That to me was success.

And oddly enough.

I.

Was.

Satisfied.

Take 5 with Dr. Rap

What and why are your purpose and your mission.
How and when are your plan and your vision.
Before you do the how, you've got to claim the what.
Without a why, you just can't how.

Remember that the quickest way is not necessarily the best way.
Check out the terrain.
See what you are facing.
Hills.
Mud.
Rain.
Sun.
Enemies.
Work.
Sweat.
Clouds.
Rocks.
Fire.
Jealousy.
Adversity.
Valleys.
Plains.
Failures.
Successes.
Forests.
Rivers.
Competition.
Exams.
Challenges.
Hardships.
Victories.
Surprises.
The terrain is not flat.
It has a few bumps.
Your road is not 100% cruise control.
If it is, you're on the wrong road.
The obstacles are not uncommon.
In fact they are too common.

Formulate your plan.
Keep your map by your side.
Be prepared for the unexpected.
Be ready to make minor and major adjustments.
Get your gear in order.
Guard your heart.
Reward yourself for meeting your checkpoints.
Go back and answer the question "what is your purpose and why"
if you haven't done so.
And Bon Voyage!

Section III

Pursuit

The woods are lovely, dark and deep.
But I have promises to keep,
And miles to go before I sleep,
And miles to go before I sleep.

—Robert Frost
"Stopping by Woods on a Snowy Evening"

-20-

Go to the Ball

Pursuit of a goal.
No matter who says what.
It's not easy.
Playing in the NBA was a boyhood dream.
But basketball.
Was not.
For.
Me.
In retrospect, I should have tried out for the B-Team.
What was I afraid of?
To be cut the second time?
To once again face the possibility of standing on the sidelines and
feeling shame?
To be known as one of the two who didn't make it?
To sit in class amongst athletes, and feel insignificant?
To fail once again?
Yes.
Yes to all the questions.
But that was yesterday.
And the mistake I made by quitting belongs to yesterday.
And today is today.
That's all I've got.
"I should have, would have, could have" is buried under ground.
I learned from my mistakes.
I learned from my failures.
And from those days spent in the gym, where the sun's soft rays
would strike the windows ever so gently, I learned many lessons.

I've learned that at times, no matter how strong the will, there are physical limitations which define my humanity.

I've learned that basketball is a recreational blast instead of unpleasant drills.

Though I never played basketball on a high school team, I have learned many lessons in this game that are ingrained in my soul and applied in my daily life.

And for these lessons I thank the coach whom I once resented, if not hated.

When the ball was thrown to me in practice, I was constantly taught one essential rule.

"Go to the ball."

"Sam, the ball is not going to come to you! You must go to the ball!"

Go to the ball.

Make the effort.

Jump.

Leap.

Dive.

Hustle.

Soar.

Go.

Go after your dream.

Pursue it.

Breathe it.

Visualize it.

Live it.

See it.

Hear it.

Embrace it.

Tackle it.
Get it.
Go!
Go to the ball!
I also learned not only to hear, but to listen.
I learned that I was not meant to be someone else.
I was not meant to be Dr. J.
I was meant to be myself.
My calling was to heal.
Heal the hearts.
Heal the souls.
And whatever come may.
I wasn't going to let any coach or counselor throw me off this team and steal my dream.
I had worn out those kitchen chairs more ways than one.
Hours were dedicated daily sitting on them and pounding out homework.
The dream to be in the NBA died.
But the dream to heal grew with an unquenchable flame.

Wherever you are in life, go to the ball!

The Good, Bad & Ugly

Two teachers have impacted me greatly.
Mr. O'Neil encouraged me.
Mr. Z. (not real initial) discouraged me.
Mr. O. said I had imagination.
Mr. Z. said I memorized too much.
Mr. O. gave me self worth.
Mr. Z. gave me a complex.
Mr. O. praised my strengths.
Mr. Z. mocked my weaknesses.
Mr. O. compelled me to do better.
Mr. Z. suppressed me with his ridicule.
One lifted.
The other crushed.
One believed in me.
The other didn't.
One said I can dream.
The other said I can't.
Both influenced me greatly.
Day in.
And day out.
Week after week.
Month after month.
Trimester after trimester.
I heard both of them.
I heard the good.
I heard the bad.
I saw the ugly.
And I chose what I wanted to choose.

-22-

Disabling the Disability

Disabilities and adversities are inevitable.
And, at times, they are present to be overcome.
For instance, cripple him, and you have a Sir Walter Scott.
Lock him in a prison cell, and you have a John Bunyan.
Bury him in the snows of Valley Forge, and you have a
George Washington.
Raise him in abject poverty, and you have an Abraham Lincoln.
Strike him down with infantile paralysis, and he becomes
Franklin D. Roosevelt.
Burn him so severely in a schoolhouse fire that the doctors say he will
never walk again, and you have a Glenn Cunningham, who set a
world's record in 1934 for running a mile in 4 minutes, 6.7 seconds.
Have him or her born black in a society filled with racial discrimina-
tion, and you have a Booker T. Washington, a Harriet Tubman, a
Marian Anderson, or a George Washington Carver.
Make him the first child to survive in a poor Italian family of eighteen
children, and you have an Enrico Caruso.
Call him a slow learner, "retarded," and write him off as ineducable,
and you have an Albert Einstein.
Deafen a genius composer, and you have a Ludwig Van Beethoven.

What were you saying about your last string?

-23-

Messn' with my Mind

Most of us don't ask for much.
Just a few words.
But constant feedback doesn't exist.
Nor is it needed.
My teacher Mr. Z. constantly said, "You have no imagination… you like to memorize too much."
Why?
Why say it?
Why destroy?
Why discourage?
Why give someone a complex?
Why not build instead?
Why not protect?
Why not encourage?
Why not uplift?
Why not strengthen?
Why not tell the truth in a gentle way?
I don't know.
Maybe some people need to make themselves appear better by mocking others.
Whatever.
I didn't believe Mr. Z.
I heard him.
But I didn't listen to him.

Oddly enough I chose to learn from him.

For he taught me a great lesson.

One of the basic needs of a human being is the need to be appreciated.

One of the kindest things we can do to a person is to give a warm smile.

One of the blessings in life is to receive an encouraging letter or kind words from a friend.

If you don't think so...

Your heavy and calloused heart can use a little love.

By Permission of Johnny Hart and Creators Syndicate, Inc.

-24-

It's your Day Mary Kay

During the Great Depression, she was a widow raising small children in Houston, Texas.

Selling Stanley brushes, she could barely feed her family.

She desperately wanted to attend the yearly national business convention held in Dallas, Texas, but needed $12 for a three-night stay in the hotel.

Her friends told her to get a real job and start supporting her family. Instead, she borrowed the $12 and went to Dallas.

She arrived, having set her goal at meeting incredibly productive and successful salespeople, hoping to learn their secrets.

For three days, she had crackers and cheese for breakfast, lunch and dinner because she couldn't afford anything else.

On the eve of the final day, the "Queen of Sales" was honored.

Mary Kay, the widow from Houston, had spent three days following the "Queen," asking questions, and learning from the best.

Mary Kay had even convinced the "Queen" to put on a mock sales party so she could learn from her.

That night, Mr. Stanley Beverage, the CEO, was present handing out awards.

Mr. Beverage shook the hands of all the lady salespeople.

Mary Kay was in the middle of the pack, waiting in line.

When her turn came, she looked Mr. Beverage intently in the eye and said, "Mr. Beverage, you don't know who I am, but next year this time you will... because I am going to be the 'Queen of Sales.'"

Mr. Beverage could have brushed her off, by saying, "Everyone says that."

But he didn't.

He calmly gazed into her eyes and said, "You know, young lady, somehow or other, I believe you will."

Those words had a profound impact on her life.

And Mary Kay never once thought about quitting.

Playing on her last string, with cheese, crackers, twelve dollars and no support, she gave all she had.

And the next year...

The "Queen of Sales" was no other than Mary Kay.

-25-

No Despair

At times people will leave you.
Don't be helpless.
At times hope will seem to flee.
Don't be hopeless.
At times happiness will desert you.
Don't despair.
At times there will be no light.
Don't be blinded.
Don't turn back.
Don't give in.
Don't give up.
Don't stop short.
Even if you find yourself lost in the valley of a thousand midnights.
Fight.
Sweat.
Fall.
Get back up.
Use wisdom.
Use experience.
Ask for help.
Look within.
Look around.
Look above.
There will be hope.
There will be light.
There will be life.

But it seems that we don't enjoy adversity.
We don't like to be placed under great pressure.
We don't like to go under the fire.
Did you know that the finest china in the world is burned at least three times?
Why does it go through that intense fire?
Once ought to be enough.
Twice should do the job.
No.
Three times are necessary to burn that china so that the sparkling gold and the beautiful crimson colors are masterfully displayed.
Are you going through the fire?
Are your strings about to snap?
Just remember.
Through it all.
Through the heat.
And through the fire.
You are being prepared to shine.

-26-

The Pass-Fail Jitters

College years came by fast.
Not easy to be a rookie.
Freshman year.
First class.
First day.
Me.
I felt alone.
A complete unknown.
In a huge auditorium.
With about five hundred students.
I was in the halls of "great" education, whatever that is.
The professor was a bearded man.
He seemed to be a creature of habit, having taught over twenty
years.
Same transparencies.
Same diagrams.
Same coffee-stained and sun-pruned biology notes.
And the same dullness that resonated from his mouth into our
fearful hearts.
Would I pass?
Would I fail?
Was I in the right class?
"Why are there so many people in this class? And what's the deal
with everybody in the university taking this course?" I thought to
myself.
The professor wrapped the microphone around his neck, and asked,
"How many of you in this class are aspiring doctors?"
I looked to the left.
I looked to the right.

In front.
And behind.
Everyone's hands were raised.
Everyone's!
Everyone had a dream.
Everyone wanted to become a doctor.
Everyone would work hard.
Everyone would strive.
Everyone would study.
Everyone would race.
"I hate to say this, guys," the professor continued, "but only about thirty of you will make it."
Thirty?
Only thirty?
Flag.
And not just a flag.
Red flag.
Alarms.
Going off in my head.
"This is hard Sam.
This is going to be hard Sam."
He was lecturing.
About some plants.
I was thinking.
About my future.
"Thirty?
Only thirty?
Stop.
Stop Sam.
Listen.
Listen to the professor.
Get the notes down.
It's OK.

Just listen.
Just write.
Just concentrate.
OK.
'Oh, God, help me please!'
Come on Sam, concentrate."
The race had begun.
My journey had started.
I never would have guessed what was to follow.
But I was well on my way.
Long road ahead.
Robert Frost had nailed it in the poem, "Stopping by Woods on a Snowy Evening."
    "The woods are lovely, dark and deep.
    But I have promises to keep.
    And miles to go before I sleep.
    And miles to go before I sleep."

Safe journey.
God speed.

Carbon Bond

My courses usually had lectures and labs.
I hated Chemistry.
I don't know why.
Perhaps because it came so easy to some.
And seemed impossible for me.
Organic chemistry was the worst!
It drove me absolutely insane.
Rings, equations, carbons and arrows were only followed by more rings, carbons, and arrows.
I don't use that stuff today when I walk into a patient's room.
I don't tell my patients that their heart is failing because their carbons are all messed up.
"Yes, Mr. Smith, it's that carbon bond that caused the heart attack… "
But I had to take it.
You know, in life, sometimes we don't get what we want.
And sometimes we get what we don't want.
Life has its obstacles.
At times there is no escaping them.
Detours are not always available.
Just straight-ahead baby.
No ignoring.
No passing 'Go.'
Just straight-ahead.
Get your fierce bulldozer attitude in gear.
And charge.
Charge hard.
And charge till the obstacle falls.
It's like that…
Know what I'm sayn'?

-28-

Balanced Out

In the course of my freshman year, I changed my major from
Biology to Psychobiology.
Little bit of Psychology.
Little bit of Biology.
Too much of one thing drives me crazy.

Balance.
Have a balance in life.
Extremes don't work.
Inflexibility shows no character.
I, for one, need to learn how to be more accommodating.
To change at times.
Not my honor.
Not my morals.
And not so much my beliefs.
But in tough situations.
I need to learn how to change.
And better myself.

Dizzy Diver

Balance is essential.

And vertigo can knock you out.

Vertigo is a sense of dizziness, as if the room is spinning out of control, leaving the person in complete terror.

At times the cause is a viral ear infection.

But at times, an etiology[1] is not found, baffling both the physician as well as the distraught patient.

A bag of tricks full of vertigo used on a high diver would be a cruel joke.

But that's exactly what hit Mary Ellen Clark, two-time Olympic bronze-medal winner in high diving.

Vertigo first hit her in 1988.

After hitting the water like a bullet in a Southern Cross meet in Australia, she lost her orientation in the water.

She made it out of the water, but struggled with vertigo for the following five months.

After her five-month battle, her vertigo mysteriously vanished.

And she pursued her diving.

But it returned to cripple her again in 1990.

Somehow, she overcame, and made the 1992 U.S. Olympic Team.

Then, at age 29, most reporters and journalists said she was too old to win a medal.

She won the bronze.

Her passion and love for the sport inspired her to pursue another Olympic appearance.

But in 1995, after springing off the board, her vertigo returned.

---

[1] *etiology:* cause of disease.

She cancelled out of the Pan American Games that year.
Clark tried anything from Eastern remedies to Western drugs to prayer.
Finding relief through the Upledger Institute's Cranio-Sacral Therapy, she came back.
Leaping off 33-foot platforms in the 1996 summer Olympics in Atlanta, Georgia, she won her second bronze medal.
Vertigo or not.
With uncivilized reporters by her side.
She had a dream.
Even though impossible it seemed.
Her heart said she could.
And Clark pursued.

-30-

Pushing 30

If you want dizzy, look into life's windows from the ER.

Like a 15 year-old kid with a bullet in his head can show up in the emergency room because he was too hip-hop to hang out with the drug-free group.

Or a 5 year-old kid rolls in with a bullet lodged in her chest because she was playing innocently in her yard and was shot by senseless hoodlums.

Life 101 has inspired me to reach my community, and hopefully save a life—before that life, that senselessly fights over colors, territories and drugs, enters the emergency room.

You ever heard of Dr. Rap?

The rapping doctor.

That would be me.

I use rap music because that's the way I can relate my anti-violence message to the kids.

With on-site visits to schools and prisons, I talk with kids all over the U.S., warning them about the dangers of drugs and violence, and encourage them to jealously care for themselves and their neighbors.

If you want dizzy, look into life's windows from your local high school or community prison.

When speaking with the students, I've noticed that elementary kids aim high.

And many high school kids roam aimlessly.

Kids in the elementary schools want to be doctors, astronauts, teachers, singers, and scientists.

But many kids in high school have no goals or ambitions.

In fact, when asked directly about life and what is to come, many high school students don't think they will live beyond age 30!

What transforms these kids?
What happens to the smiles and laughter?
What happens to the dreams?
What happens to imagination and the purple colored cows?
Why do many of the high school students drop out?
Why do many of them attend school without being present?
Perhaps they feel unloved.
Perhaps they feel betrayed.
Perhaps they feel abandoned.
Perhaps they feel lonely.
Perhaps they feel insecure.
Perhaps they seek the truth.
Perhaps they feel a void.
Perhaps they feel angry.
Perhaps they feel lost.
Perhaps they feel cheated.
Perhaps they feel a pain, like a piece of glass cutting their soul.
Perhaps they don't have role models.
Or their role models are on drugs.
I don't have all the answers.
But I do have a solution.
These youngsters need a lot of attention and affection.
We need to spend time with these kids.
Volunteer.
Inspire them.
Challenge them.
Sacrifice for them.
Pray for them.
And give to them of our heart.
Think about it.
These youngsters will one day give to us what we give to them.

-31-

It's Your World, Baby

If you want to visit Vertigo-Land, try to get into medical school.
My counselor in Psychobiology worked hard to help me succeed.
In my junior year, the stakes were raised.
It was time for the MCATs.
The Medical College Admission Test.
I didn't know then what I know now.
Having now interviewed prospective medical school applicants,
I know that the MCAT is the most important screening tool that
medical schools utilize.
If you have 8,000 applicants.
And you have to pick 100.
You have to make some sort of distinction.
You have to set standards.
Applicants have to stand out.
And I'll tell you.
It's not your looks.
It's not your school.
It's not your hometown.
And it ain't your daddy (most of the time).
It's your MCAT score.
One score.
One test.
One day.
It doesn't matter if you're sick on the day of the exam.

If you score high.
You're basically in.
If you score low.
You're a has-been.
What about the last three years of college work?
The lectures.
The exams.
The sweat.
(Like you're sitting in a classroom, taking a test.
And the clock shrieks that you're running out of time.
All your classmates are finished and are staring at you with
one eyebrow raised.
And you?
You're still on the first question.
You start to panic.
You sweat.
Your number two pencil breaks and you don't have a spare one.
So you start using your pen to color in those obnoxious round boxes.
You look up.
You look around.
You look down.
And bury your face close to the questions.
But you can't understand the questions any more.
They're not even written in English.
They're in Chinese!
And not only did you decide to skip Chinese classes in junior high,
but this is not Kung Pao Chicken!
Oh my God!

Only a few seconds left.
The clock yells stop.
The professor hovers over your desk.
And tries to snatch the paper out of your hands.
But you are now writing frantically in what appears to be Chinese scribble.
You have now failed.
And your life is over.
Your friends turn their back to you, partly because they are ashamed of you and partly because they are embarrassed for you.
You start to cry, and yell, "I'm sorry, please help me!"
People are now laughing at you.
And just then.
Just then you wake up.
It is 2 A.M.
You are not in class.
You are in your own bed in your own bedroom.
You're soaking wet.
Your heart rate exceeds your maximum capacity.
And you are thankful that you are still alive.
And yes, tomorrow's test will be in English).
One score on one test can make a big difference.
It doesn't seem fair, does it?
But this is the real world.
Welcome to Life 101.
Live large.
And play hard.

-32-

You Got Choice

Everything in life requires dedication.
Whether studying for a test or helping the next generation.
And dedication is a choice.
Everything we do involves choices.
For instance, you and I can choose to be lazy or productive.
I don't think one is born lazy… that's his or her disposition… I believe
we choose to be lazy or productive.
You and I can choose to be happy or bitter.
You and I have a choice to be up or down.
Despite our circumstances.
Despite the reality.
Despite the hardships.
Despite the impossibility of the situation.
Despite the obstacles.
Despite what you and I face or will encounter.
We choose our attitudes.
We choose our reaction.
We choose to be bitter or joyful.
And we choose our stance.

The outside world can be harsh.
The outside world can be cold.
The outside world can be cruel.
The outside world can be unfair.
Downright ugly.
Hurting us.
Tearing us down.
Stripping our dignity.
Challenging our integrity.
Striking our honor.
Crushing our power.
But what choices have we made?
What choices are we making?
And what choices will we make?
It's up to us.
It's our move.
And it's our choice to rise above the embrace of darkness.

-33-

∿EKGs and ABCs

A good mentor teaches you the skills of his art.
But an exceptional mentor gives you insight into life.
One of my Cardiology mentors in internal medicine residency
not only taught me how to read the EKGs, but also how to live my
ABCs:

Availability.
Affability.
Ability.

Be there.
Be pleasant.
Be skilled.

Have **C**ourage: Face your weaknesses.
Have **C**ontrol: Compose yourself in a manner worthy of your calling.
Have **C**onfidence: Drop arrogance.
Have **C**oncentration: Focus.
And **C**onquer your fear: Turn your weaknesses into strengths.

Thanks Milt! (Milton Smith, MD)

Take 5 with Dr. Rap

In the 1930s a high school located in a small Oklahoma town had one of the worst football teams. They virtually were winless. Their students, teachers and the people of the town were dispirited from continual defeat, especially to their arch-rivals.

After witnessing another loss, a rich oil producer decided to take matters into his own hands. He offered to buy a new Ford for every football player and coach on the team if they won the homecoming game against their bitter rival. The team went mad! For the next seven days all they did was eat, drink and live football. The entire school and community caught the bug and cheered their team.

Finally, the big event arrived. The excitement charted off the Richter scale. The crowd held its breath in anticipation of a long awaited victory. The players dreamt of their new Fords. They huddled as a unit and spurred each other onward. They hit the field and played with passion. When the lights were turned off and all had gone home, the score was 38 to 0.

No Fords for the players.
No victory for the school.
No cure for the team.
No cheers for the coming week.

In the pursuit of your dreams, remember…
That discipline is a long-term effort.
That hard work is a lifetime commitment.
And that determination must be accompanied with a relentless drive for excellence.

Section IV

Perseverance

When you get to the end of your rope,
tie a knot and hang on.

—Franklin D. Roosevelt
32nd President of the United States

-34-

There Ain't No

There ain't no:
Perfect job.
Perfect house.
Perfect marriage.
Perfect person.
Perfect situation.
Perfect circumstance.
Perfect restaurant.
Perfect vacation.
Perfect car.
Perfect teacher.
Perfect mentor.
Perfect family.
Perfect child.
Perfect parent.
Perfect friend.
Perfect pet.
Perfect cellular phone.
Perfect computer.
Perfect gadget.
Perfect internet host.
Perfect sound system.
Perfect college.
Perfect (non-fat) ice cream.

Take what you've got.
And work with it.
  —Dr. Rap

-35-

Reject

The MCAT (Medical College Admissions Test) is the most obnoxious standardized test on earth.
Of this I am convinced.
Too many questions.
So little time.
I spent months preparing.
Jammed in all the biology, chemistry and physics I could in the empty crevices of my brain.
I took the test and thought I did well.
The results were supposed to be back in six to eight weeks.
It came in the tenth week.
It made no difference for me to run outside every day to check the mail, starting the fifth week.
Open.
Hold my breath.
Check the mail.
No results.
Close the box.
Disappointed, but breathing.
You've been there, haven't you?
The torture lies in waiting for the results.
And I finally received my scores.
Yes!
This was it.
Medicine world, start to embrace me!

It would be insane to prepare all your life for a mission, and then have one set of scores strip your dreams away from you.

My applications were already sent to nine medical schools.

Questions were all answered on the primary and secondary application forms… why do you want to be medical doctor… why our school… why now… who influenced you most… what are your strengths… what are your weaknesses???

School after school.

Check after check.

I had filled everything out.

All the schools were waiting for my scores.

And then came the responses from medical schools.

They had received my scores.

Letter by letter.

Addressed to me.

"Dear Mr. Kojoglanian… we are sorry to inform you that… "

Nine applications.

Nine rejections.

No acceptance letters.

No acceptance speeches.

No blue ribbons.

And no fulfilled dreams.

-36-

Crossroads

There I was.
A senior in college.
Getting a degree in Psychobiology.
But no acceptance to medical school.
I had been turned down.
I remembered having studied many nights and feeling guilty
for sleeping.
I remembered having a counselor tell me that I would
never make it.
I remembered closing my eyes and feeling the failure
choking my soul.
I remembered having sat in the huge auditorium as a freshman.
In that Biology class.
Where a professor of Science greeted the rookies.
He had asked who planned to go to medical school.
All 500 students raised their hands.
"By the end of your senior year... only 30 of you will make it."
Sure enough!
Many of my friends had changed their career goals.
Many had dropped out of the sciences.
Only a handful had made it into medical school.

I felt defeated.
I felt inadequate.
I felt cheated.
I felt angry.
In the pursuit, I had come across two counselors.
One was the director in Psychobiology.
He encouraged me.
Told me I could make it.
Another is to be unnamed.
He discouraged me.
And told me that I don't have what it takes to become a medical doctor.
Do I quit?
Or do I try again?
Crossroads.
Tough times.
Tough decisions.
Tough life.

-37-

Re-Do

Have you ever failed?
Have you ever fallen?
Have you ever experienced a setback?
Have you ever been told you don't have what it takes?
As you read this line, have you given up on your dreams?
Can I give you this advice?
Re-focus.
Re-plan.
Re-think.
Re-bound.
Re-direct.
Re-gain.
Re-start.
Re-try.
Re-claim.
Re-calculate.
Re-fuel.
Re-charge.
Re-commit.
Re-examine.
Re-apply.
Re-adapt.
Re-adjust.

Re-allocate.
Re-evaluate.
Re-arrange.
Re-attempt.
Re-energize.
Re-set.
Re-strengthen.
Re-kindle.
Re-test.
Re-equip.
Re-fortify.
Re-organize.
Re-tool.
Re-train.
Re-dedicate.
And just re-do it again!
   —Dr. Rap

-38-

Reject, with a Twist

Senior year in college.
Four-year schedule completed.
Plans pursued with precision.
All the requirements met.
I was to graduate on time.
My Bachelor of Science was earned.
But I had failed to make it into medical school.
I have heard motivation speakers say that they have never failed;
they have just "experienced set-backs."
How nice.
Let's just call it what it is, and move on.
I failed to get into medical school.
I had heard that USC (The University of Southern California School
of Medicine, now known as the Keck School of Medicine of the
University of Southern California) offered a masters program in
Anatomy, where a select few take courses side by side with medical
students.
If these students excelled in the masters program, they could apply
to the medical school.
So I tried.
I applied.
There were 30 some odd applicants for 3 spots.
I was told that I was the fourth to be picked.
Fourth?
Missed it by one?
Denied again?
Senior year coming to an end.
And I had no job.

I had no clue.
I had no time.
What was I to do?
Quit?
Just like the "Dr. J" dream?
Like the kitchen chairs?
Like the varsity basketball team?
Like the two young men standing on the sidelines, having been cut from the team?
I asked one of the professors in the masters program if he would let me take a class as a "special student status."
Long shot.
But a try.
An attempt to stay afloat.
An attempt to rise above my sorry circumstances.
An attempt to stare at failure, search for lost courage, and strive without looking defeated.
I sat in the professor's office.
He checked my files.
My scores.
My grades.
My records.
My letters.
My essays.
He looked at me and asked.
"So why do you think I should let you in?"
"I will work hard sir. Please give me a chance. I will work with all my heart and strength, and will not disappoint you."
He was quiet.
He looked through my files again.

Page after page.

Was he really reading that stuff?

I don't know.

I just sat and prayed, asking for God's help.

"We'll give you a try. You can take Gross Anatomy and Micro Anatomy with the medical students this semester, and we'll see how you do."

A ray of hope!

A journey with obstacles.

But none the less, a journey with hope.

"Thank you sir. Thank you."

I walked out of the office.

No medical school.

No masters.

No job.

No major promises.

No clear victories.

No easy road maps.

No celebrations.

But hope.

And at that desperate moment, when doubt marred my vision and fear chained my mind, the "special student status" sounded like double platinum!

-39-

What the Golf Ball Don't Know

Mark O'Meara.
41 years old in 1998.
Professional golfer.
18 year career.
56 majors played.
No wins.
Until...
April 1998: victory at the Masters.
July 1998: victory at the British Open.
It doesn't matter whether you like golf or not.
That's not my point.
The fact is that this man kept on playing despite his past accomplishments.
When asked about his age, he replied, "The golf ball doesn't know how old you are."
Yo, check it out.
No matter what the odds.
No matter what the past.
No matter what the record.
Four strings or down to the last.
Don't give in.
Don't quit.
Don't stop.
Don't despair.
Strive.
Search.
Stand.
Strike.
Soar above all limits.
Reach your dreams.
And go beyond!

-40-

Dissecting the Dead

First day.
In medical school.
Not as a medical student.
But as a "special status student."
The auditorium was packed.
130 students.
Most were there as first year medical students.
They too had taken the journey.
And they had arrived.
I looked intently in their eyes and faces.
I desperately searched for clues to help me understand what was different about them.
How did they manage to overcome?
How did they conquer and achieve?
What did it take?
They too aspired.
They too studied.
They too planned.
But they were there as medical students.

Side by side, we took Gross Anatomy (dissecting dead bodies to learn every muscle, bone, ligament, tendon, artery, nerve and vein in the human anatomy).
Side by side we studied.
Side by side we took our exams.
Side by side we endured.
And side by side we excelled.
It didn't matter to them whether I was a medical student or a "special status student."
And after a while, it didn't matter to me.
I felt like I too belonged.
The more I studied, the more I knew that medicine was for me.
And no matter what come may...
There was no height.
No depth.
No width.
No obstacle.
That could stop me from trying to reach my dream.

-41-

Re-Apply

While taking the medical school courses, I prepared for the MCATs,
and began to reapply to medical schools once again.
The first process had shut me out.
Nine applications.
With nine rejections.
This second time, I applied to 18 schools.
Took the MCATs.
And waited.
Waited for good news.
Waited for an acceptance letter.
Waited patiently.
Waited with great expectations.
The MCATs hadn't changed much.
Still obnoxious.
Still long.
And still hard.
And I?
Maybe a bit more humble.
Maybe a bit wiser.
Maybe a bit more knowledgeable.
And like that little boy playing football for the first time on American
soil… perhaps a bit thrown off… but with an unquenchable dream.

DENNIS THE MENACE

"JUST BE THANKFUL HE DOESN'T WALK ON ALL FOURS."

-42-

Route 30's Clearview

William Powell set out to do the impossible in the 1940s.

He was a man who spent four years in the army, serving America in World War II.

He was a man who had a passion for his family.

A man who loved golf, but was not welcomed to play in the local golf courses because of the color of his skin.

It was then when this security guard from Ohio made a choice.

Instead of reasoning with the unreasonable.

Instead of complaining.

Instead of becoming bitter.

Instead of begging.

He took action.

One afternoon, while driving down Route 30, he saw an old 78-acre dairy farm for sale, and proclaimed to his wife that this was the site of his own golf course.

He applied for a GI loan.

He was turned down.

Everyone seemed to be getting loans except colored veterans, he thought.

Ultimately his brother and two black doctors helped him buy the land.

Some people told him that he had lost his mind.

Some said, "It takes big money to do what you're trying to do. You'll never make it."

But Mr. Powell knew in his heart that this place on Route 30 would be one where he and his children could play and be welcomed at the same time.

He walked the farm many times.

He studied the terrain intently.

And then sat down at the kitchen table and laid out his plans.

He leveled hills and formed new contours with earthmovers.

Laying in the fairways and greens was no mystery to this man who had picked up a lot of lawn-care knowledge from his early golfing days.

He planted blue spruce, maple, crab apple, dogwood and oaks.

He dug water holes and set up the tees for nine holes.

And in 1948, he proudly announced the opening of Clearview Golf Course.

Though the response was overwhelmingly positive, there were days when he had to deal with tire ruts on some of the greens and stolen flagsticks.

It would be 13 more years before the Professional Golfers' Association of America allowed blacks to play on their tours.

In 1967, his daughter went on tour with the Ladies Professional Golf Association, playing for 13 years. Her victories included winning the Kelly Springfield Open in Australia.

In the early 1970s, he repaid his two doctor friends, and turned around and bought 52 adjacent acres so he could expand the course to 18 holes.

Now in his eighties, Mr. Powell goes out onto his fairway in a golf cart and sits and savors the beauty.

He stares at the American flag fluttering in the wind.

And gives thanks for the strength he had to realize his dream and the wisdom to fulfill it.

-43-

Interview Skills
& the Lack Thereof

Medical School was a trip.
New students.
Old professors.
Gross Anatomy with dead bodies.
Micro Anatomy with microscopes and minute organisms.
I studied day and night.
To prove to myself.
To prove to the professors.
To prove to the school.
That I could make it.
Two elements make things happen.
Attitude.
An immutable attitude.
And Work.
Hard work.
And I went all out.
At the same time, I was waiting to hear from the 18 medical schools
that I applied to several months before.
The letters came in.
One by one.
Saying how flooded they were with applications.
And how I did not meet their standards because this year's applicants
were so competitive.
Finally.
After receiving the 14th rejection letter, I was granted an interview.
Finally.

I could prove myself.

Live and in color.

Nothing could stop me.

I was asked the question, "What would you do if you did not make it into medical school?"

"Well, I would probably try counseling… it deals with people's emotions… and I feel that I can be comforting to those who hurt."

Hello!

Counseling?

Nothing wrong with being a counselor.

My sister is a great counselor.

But that's not who I am.

And that's not who I was meant to be.

"If the doors are slammed in my face… and there is no hope left… if the rejection letters keep pouring in… I will guarantee you one thing… I will not quit… I will stand tall… I will learn from my mistakes… and correct them… I will work harder… I will strive… and I will knock on the doors of medicine until someone opens them wide!"

Yes, that's what I should have said… but didn't.

Letter 15: I didn't get into that school.

The letters came through the mail.

Letter 16.

Letter 17.

Letter 18.

All the same.

And all with one theme.

Rejection.

Rejection.

Rejection.

-44-

De-Reject This

I may be hard pressed
But I am not crushed.

I may be perplexed,
But I am not in despair.

I may be afflicted
But I am not abandoned.

I may be struck down
But I am not destroyed.

I chose not to quit.
You can laugh.
You can mock.
You can try to intimidate.
You can try to discourage.
You can throw me out.
You can shut all doors.
But I chose not to quit.
I chose.
Not to quit.

-45-

Defeating Defeat

Lost his job in 1832.
Defeated for the legislature in 1832.
Failed in business and went broke in 1833.
Elected to the legislature in 1834.
Sweetheart died in 1835.
Had a nervous breakdown in 1836.
Defeated for the Speaker of the House in 1838.
Defeated for the nomination to the Congress in 1843.
Elected to the Congress in 1846.
Lost his re-nomination in 1848.
Rejected for Land Officer in 1849.
Defeated for the Senate in 1854.
Defeated for nomination of the Vice Presidency in 1856.
Once again defeated for the Senate in 1858.
If this were someone's batting average in baseball, it would be 0.143 (not good).
Next time up.
1860.
At the plate.
Bat in hand.
Ball pitched.
Forget the 0.143 average.
He never gave up.
And he's elected President of the United States.
Grand Slam by Abraham Lincoln.

You never know where the next opportunity will take you.
Get your bat ready.
Keep your eye on the ball.
And no matter how many times you strike out...
Swing!

-46-

Shake & Bake that Cake

Charlie Lubin made great cheesecake.
It was so good that he thought of opening a cheesecake store.
And so he did on the north side of Chicago.
Business went so well that he decided to open a second store in
South Chicago.
That store was such a disaster, that Lubin ended up losing both
stores.
He sat in his house one day and ate a cheesecake he had made.
"This is good cheesecake!" he exclaimed, and decided to open up his
store again.
Success was once again his, and he opened up the second store.
But once again, both stores were shut down.
A few months later, while eating his prized cheesecake, he said, "This
is good cheesecake!"
And you guessed it.
He opened a cheesecake store again.
And after opening a second store, he went bankrupt again.
History repeated itself for a total of four times.
Months later, Lubin was eating his own cheesecake.
And you know what he said, "This is good cheesecake!"
You also know what he did.
To tell you the truth, I don't even think he had any strings left!
He opened up another store.
Only this time, he named the cheesecake store after his daughter's
name, Sara Lee.
That would be... Sara Success Lee.

-47-

Teach 'em Teacher

Two years in a row.
27 rejections later.
I was unable to gain admission to medical school.
My "special student status" year was about to expire.
Then where would I go?
Out of desperation, I applied to the Anatomy Masters program again.
I'm not sure how many applicants they received that time around.
But it didn't matter.
I got in.
I got in and was asked, "Would you like to teach Gross Anatomy to the medical students as a teaching assistant?"
Would I be interested?
Hello!!
"When can I start?"
"The beginning of the new school year."
There I was.
A reject that was officially to begin his masters program.
And this reject was to teach medical students?
Life has its moments.
And life has its miracles.
Check the scoreboard.
27 applications.
27 rejections.
2 years worth of attempts.
2 of those rejections came from Keck School of Medicine of the University of Southern California.
The first in 1988.
And the second in 1989.

And in 1989, I was to teach Gross Anatomy to medical students at Keck School of Medicine of the University of Southern California.
Are you with me?
You feeln' this?
You understand the irony?
You understand the insane situation?
I'm about to teach medical students in a school I can't get into.
You feel it, right?
Call it what you'd like.
To me, this was a miracle.
And I went all out.
I studied harder than before.
I studied the muscles.
Studied the joints.
Studied the nerves.
And their incredible course through the body.
Their function.
Book after book.
Mnemonic after mnemonic.
Point after point.
I explained with passion.
I taught with zeal.
I gave my all.
And the students responded.
They asked for review sessions before exams.
And I gave it to 'em.
I even took part in setting up questions for the exams!
I smile as I work on this document on my PC.
I smile because of the crazy odds.
The odds of teaching in one of the schools that had rejected me two years in a row!
The odds of a boy who was pushed down the stairs in elementary school and was told to "Go home, you foreigner," to be teaching in medical school.

The odds of one who "memorized too much."
The odds of one who was told by a counselor, "You don't have what it takes."
I did not apply to medical school that year.
The masters program was a gift from God.
I wanted to complete the program.
I therefore focused on finishing the masters program and kept teaching.
As a student, I studied religiously.
As a teacher, I taught passionately.
As a person, I grew tremendously.
The roads and crossways on the journey were not as I had imagined.
Perhaps I thought the roads would be straighter.
That the ground would be firmer.
That the obstacles would not be so numerous.
That there would be more help along the way.
That dreaming is in itself achieving.
How I was mistaken!
The journey is not so easy.
And the goal reached is not necessarily the time to celebrate.
However, each step seems to be a miracle of its own.
Each small increment seems to be an achievement in and of itself.
There are times of despair.
Times of failure.
Times of hope.
Times of setback.
Times of rest.
Times of more work.
And times of celebration.
Each day is a journey.
Each moment is an opportunity.
And each second is a gift.

-48-

Reject Again?

The first year as a special status student was over.
The next year as an official master's student had come to a
quick end.
The third and last year in the masters had begun.
I continued taking the required courses in the masters program.
At the same time, I took courses with the medical students, which
not only counted towards my masters but also was credited
towards medical school.
I also kept on teaching Gross Anatomy.
I applied again to medical school.
This time, only to one school, an early decision track.
To the Keck School of Medicine of the University of Southern
California, where I was a teaching assistant.
Early decision is not an easy process.
You apply early only to one school.
If you make it, you're informed much earlier than other applicants.
If you don't, you have plenty of time to apply to other schools for
the same year.
I applied.
And waited.
I was told that the committee wanted to re-review my files at a
later date.
But there was an advocate in the room, Mrs. Althea Alexander.
Someone who got up and said, "Listen, this kid has been with us
for three years. He's taught our own students. The students love him.
His professors recommend him. Now stop putting him on hold,
and just accept him."
You believe in angels?
You believe in friends?
You believe in timing?

Althea is the director of minority students at Keck School of Medicine of the University of Southern California.
Althea is a friend.
She had seen thousands of students come in and out of school.
She believed in me.
And she would not be silenced.
Friends.
They comfort.
They cheer.
They protect.
And they take a stand for us.
How blessed I was to have that friend in the front lines, fighting for me!
The committee listened to her advice.
I don't know the exact vote count.
I don't even care.
Whatever it was, it was good enough.
Wait up.
Check it out.
Before you think this is just a hop-skip and a jump away to medical school acceptance...
You remember the MCATs?
Most people take it once.
Some have to take it twice.
Did I mention to you?
That I sat through that hellish test five times.
That's probably a record.
Who knows?
Who cares!
Perseverance, attitude and hard-working habits all served me well.

If your situation is grim.
I want to remind you of one thing.
That there is still hope.
In the darkest moment, there is still hope.
Get the violin out and don't mind the broken strings.
Play your music on that one string.
Play with passion.
Play with poise.
And no matter what.
Play with soul!

-49-

Soar Beyond

Gaining acceptance into medical school was not my dream.
In retrospect, gaining acceptance was a means to ultimately reach my dreams.
I believe in setting goals.
But many times, when we reach those goals, we stop dreaming.
We stop achieving.
We stop imagining.
We stop creating.
We stop giving.
We stop trying.
We stop preparing.
And somehow, we become complacent.
Complacency breeds laziness.
And laziness breeds failure.
Remember.
Set your goals.
Soar above all limits.
Reach your dreams.
And go BEYOND!

Take 5 with Dr. Rap

Look back

> Only to remember your mission and your dreams.
> The danger of looking back is if you are successful, you might get indifferent.
> And if you are failing, you might get disheartened.
> Look back only to remember your humble beginnings.
> Look back only to find out your motivations.
> Look back only to see that you're actually moving forward.

Look ahead

> And keep your sight on your dreams.
> The danger of looking ahead is that if you concentrate on obstacles, you may fall.
> And if you detach yourself from those around you, you may lose reality.
> Look ahead and be excited about what your future holds.
> Look ahead and prepare for what is to come.
> Look ahead and march with determination.

Look where you are

> And go one step at a time.
> The danger of looking where you are is that you may think you have not come far.
> And if you start looking where you are, you may start to pity yourself.
> Look where you are and ask for help.
> Look where you are and celebrate the small victories.
> Look where you are and turn your weaknesses into your strengths.

And trash the word "quit"!

Section V

Priorities

No matter how hard the climb,
priorities
arrange the rungs of a ladder
in such a way
that great accomplishments
become inevitable.

—Samuel A. Kojoglanian, MS, MD

-50-

Turning 50

Every 7.5 seconds in this nation, someone turns 50 years old.
Perspectives begin to shift.
Values rearrange.
Waistlines expand.
And hope becomes a powerful ally.
Corporations that you devoted your whole life to, turn their backs
without giving it a second thought.
Materialism, your so-called friend, turns out to betray you.

What is important to us?
What takes center stage?
Do we have something or someone to die for?
Because if for me to live is money,
Then to die is to leave it all behind.
If for me to live is fame,
Then to die is to be soon forgotten.
If for me to live is power,
Then to die is to lose it all.
If for me to live is possessions,
Then to die is to take none of it with me.
Caskets are narrow.
Can't take anything with you.
Even if you do.
Can't use it.
You ever see a U-Haul tagged to a hearse in a funeral procession?

You will soon find that nothing can take place of family, friends and faith.
Don't figure this one out too late.
Find out now.
Look.
And see.
Hear.
And listen.
Seek.
And find.
Focus.
And if needed, make changes.
And make them now.

DENNIS THE MENACE

"...AND I'M IN MY LATE FIVES."

-51-

Dr. Rap's ABCs

Always strive to improve.
Be courteous to everyone.
Choose to be happy and find happiness by being content.
Don't flatter or kiss-up to anyone.
Edify everyone.
Flexibility wins out.
Give of your all, especially when you are not being watched.
Hug your loved ones and friends.
Invest in the lives of people.
Just get up, stop making excuses and take that first step.
Know your limitations.
Learn to say "no" kindly.
Make your bed every morning.
Never start smoking.
Own a computer and learn to use the internet.
Pray hard.
Quit smoking if you ignored "Never start smoking."
Re-try after you fail.
Smooth things out by being the first to say, "I'm sorry, I was wrong."
Treat everyone with utmost dignity, no matter what your or their
     positions may be.
Use your imagination and don't let *nobody* take away your dreams.
Visit the ocean side on a regular basis.
Watch the sun set.
Xerox your valuable documents or scan them onto your CD-ROM.
Yell like mad on amusement park rides.
Zone out at least five to ten minutes daily, catch a quick nap, find
     your sanity (and listen to Dr. Rap's CDs).

-52-

Thoughts & Destinies

Watch your thoughts; they become words.
Watch your words; they become actions.
Watch your actions; they become habits.
Watch your habits; they become character.
Watch your character; it becomes your destiny.
      —Frank Outlaw

-53-

Baby You're On!

First year in medical school.
The volume is intense.
The pressure is on.
Spotlight.
And you're on stage.
This ain't no dress rehearsal.
It's the real thing, baby.
And you're on!
It's the moment of truth.
As a master's student, I had walked the hallways of the medical
school for the past three years.
I had taken many of the required classes.
I had even taught in the school.
But I was still nervous.
Severe headaches plagued me for two weeks.
It felt as if someone were pulling out my right eye and jamming it
back into its socket.
I hadn't experienced headaches like this since my teenage years.
Then, I was quite the rookie on American soil.
I was scared to death of going to school and migraine headaches
plagued me as a manifestation of fear.
As a child I visited a doctor for the headaches.
He said I was an anxious youngster, and prescribed Erythromycin[1]
for me.
(Erythromycin? That ought to take care of the migraines and
anxiety?!).
The eye pain during medical school was so severe that I visited
an ophthalmologist.[2]

---

[1] *Erythromycin:* an antibiotic used to treat infections.
[2] *Opthalmologist:* an eye doctor.

After doing a complete exam, he told me it was probably stress.
"But I've been here with the medical students for three years now,"
I exclaimed.
"Yes, but you've now started medical school... believe me... that's
stressful."
The headaches resolved in the same week.
There's something about a doctor saying you're OK.
As if it clears your mind.
And pain miraculously goes away.
The days raced by.
The exams hit hard.
And I ran the course with the others.
I studied and continued teaching.
If you've seen the movies *Gross Anatomy* or *Patch Adams*, you have
some sense of the intense schedule that medical students face.
Lectures are never ending.
Books are expensive and too thick to stuff in the crevices of your
brain.
Many professors have forgotten what it means to have been a
student.
Midterms are constantly nagging at your worst fears.
A series of National Boards will have to be tackled.
Your days need more than 24 hours.
And graduation seems too far off.

-54-

Spitting in the Ocean

Third year in medical school is tackled with fear, but it's a blast.
Second year is cruel to the bone.
It has too much reading.
Too much memorization.
Too much pain.
Won't even talk about it.
I was on the hospital wards in my third year as a student physician.
The nurses know who's new in the big house.
We're the ones that wear the short white coats.
The "real" physicians wear the longer white coats.
All the pretty-haired, naive-looking, clueless student physicians,
desperately seeking help from anyone on the wards wear
short white coats.
I will always remember my first patient.
He had pneumonia.[1]
Antibiotics were on board.
But despite the medications, he still spiked fevers and showed no
signs of improvement.
A computed tomography[2] of his chest was ordered.
When things don't make sense.
Dig deep.
Original complaints are only a hint of what lurks deep inside.
His scan revealed a lung mass, most likely cancerous, which was
invading his lung.
Around the mass, he had developed the infection.
All this time we were treating the infection, but not the lung mass,
the etiology of his problems.
He refused any surgical intervention.
And refused any further medical treatment, including the antibiotics.

---

[1] *pneumonia:* an infection of the lungs where the patient has difficulty breathing.
[2] *Computed Tomography* (CT/CAT scan): machine that images soft tissue and bone.

My resident (the practicing doctor with a long white coat) insisted that he had no choice.

The patient said, "I do have a choice... this is my body... not yours."

"Well, I'm your doctor and you need surgery," the resident insisted.

"Who do you think you are... God?" the patient asked.

"I'm the doctor here," the resident argued.

"No you're not... you're not my doctor!" the patient rebelled.

And that was the end of the conversation.

One week's worth of antibiotics was like spitting in the ocean.

No amount of antibiotics could help our patient.

For a fighting chance to survive, he desperately needed a resection of the mass.

What we had offered in the past week could not cure the cancer.

The patient had enough.

And two days later, my patient died.

He died in peace.

Without being slashed open with an eager scalpel.

Without being poked for blood draws at four o'clock in the morning.

Without chemotherapy being dumped into his frail and lifeless veins.

Without fighting with the ugly face of futility.

He died with dignity.

And he taught me two powerful lessons.

In fact he helped me more than I could ever help him.

That is a strange part of medicine, but if we are ready to accept it, physicians can learn a lot from their patients... the first being humility.

My patient taught me to listen.

Listen to the patients.

Listen to their hearts.

Listen to their cry.

Listen to their request.

Listen and don't play God.

He also taught me another valuable lesson.

When you give up mentally, you die.

You die socially, psychologically, emotionally, spiritually and physically.

The mind is powerful.

When you give up in your mind...

When you say, "That's it"...

When you give in...

You give up the ghost.

And you basically give up your rights to live.

~55~

Friends & Daggers

Julius Caesar brought Rome to the pinnacle of its majestic power.
He was adored by much of Rome but despised by the powerful
Roman senate.
Men who were deeply indebted to him were the very ones who
conspired against him.
When the time came to murder Caesar, the assassins agreed that
each man would stab Caesar and therefore share the blame equally.
They converged on Caesar like hungry vile vultures and began to
stab him.
History records that Caesar fought his attackers fiercely.
Until he saw the face of Brutus.
Brutus was a member of the senate.
And he was known as Caesar's dearest friend.
Brutus the dear friend.
With a dagger in his hand.
Once Caesar saw the dagger in the hand of his friend, he lost the
will to fight.
And when Brutus plunged the dagger into the bleeding body,
Julius Caesar died.
He died from betrayal.

I don't underestimate the power of friends.
I have friends who love me.
And I've had friends who've betrayed me, dumped me, rejected
and surprised me.
Brutus will always walk the streets.
My challenge to you and me is that we walk in the path of loyalty.

-56-

Break a Leg

Tragedy struck in the ninth week of my third year medical school career.
I was in my Ob-Gyn (Obstetrics-Gynecology) rotation.

Here's a short tour of the medicine world...
You start out as a pre-medical student (usually four years).
Then you become a medical student (another four years).
The first two years of medical school are devoted to memorizing.
The latter two years are hospital based, doing short 4-6 week rotations in different disciplines of medicine such as Pediatrics, Surgery, Internal Medicine, Psychiatry, Obstetrics, etc. Though you wear a short white coat, at least it's a coat.
By the time you graduate from medical school, you need to have passed two national boards, the first being at the end of the second year and the latter test before graduation.
Your first year as a doctor, you are called an Intern (the rookie).
You enroll in a program such as Ob-Gyn, Surgery, Internal Medicine, Psychiatry...
And yes, since you the man (or woman), you get the *long* white coat.
In your second year as a doctor, you are known as a Resident.
After residency, you can practice as an attending (a real doctor... usually no white coat).
If you want to sub-specialize, you become a fellow (a real doctor, but still training).
You can be a fellow in Cardiology, Pulmonary, Renal and so forth.

I had just passed my first national boards and started my rotations as a third year medical student.

I was on call on a Saturday in my Ob-Gyn rotation, and didn't get any sleep.
It was a rough night with sick patients.
Patients with high fevers.
Patients with severe nausea.
All night long and no rest.
There was hardly any privacy for the patients.
A curtain separated one body from the next.
And the stench of nasty bacteria was overwhelmingly nauseating.
My intern coached me on how to draw blood, and where to send it.
Rounding on patients the next day was quick, and I was out by 10 A.M.
By 4 P.M. that day I was back in the Emergency Room.
Not with my short white coat and name badge.
Not as a student physician.
But as a patient.
The doctor came in and told me that I probably have cancer!
Cancer?
Wait up.
I was fine in the morning.
I was fine the day prior to this incident.
And now I probably have cancer?

Life is just a bit on the uncertain side.
We never plan for certain things.
You never put on the calendar that you plan to have the flu on a certain day.
Or that you'll have an emergent appendectomy.[1]
Or you'll be diagnosed with diabetes[2] on this day.
Do you sit down and calculate that you'll have a loved one diagnosed with cancer in the next year?
Or you'll lose your child.
Or you'll be in a car accident.
Or you'll get the cancellation letter from the insurance company.
No one in their right frame of mind wishes for or plans these things.
And I hadn't either.

That Sunday afternoon, I was at a picnic.
I was playing softball.

---

[1] *appendectomy:* removal of the appendix.
[2] *diabetes:* a disease in which the blood sugar is too high.

Standing in the outfield.

Soaking in the sun.

Celebrating the savored moments as a gift to enjoy the great outdoors.

My friend blasted the softball over my reach.

And I was chasing the ball.

An inconspicuous ravine in the field would set the stage for the drama that would literally change the course of my life.

With my right leg stretched before me, I scooped the ball in my glove, but was unable to negotiate the big dip in the field.

Have you ever misjudged a step while going down stairs?

You think there is one more step, but there really isn't.

And when you hit the concrete, you find yourself a little off balance and a bit surprised.

You add a little swing to your step to cover up your pitiful clumsiness.

And then add a little smile to your surprised face so if anyone were watching you, they'd think you got it goin' on!

My right foot should have hit the ground.

But it didn't because of the ravine.

And when the right leg touched down, it made an uncharacteristic sound.

My right leg gave way like the snap of a twig that is overpowered by a cruel winter's overwhelming winds.

I hit the ground.

And could not move.

I told myself that all is well.

But I knew otherwise.

I thought I might have torn my knee ligaments.

But my right thigh began to swell.

And I knew what had happened.

My friends hovered over me and told me to get up.

"Call 911," I said.

"That's like 500 bucks," one exclaimed.

"Who cares... just call 911."

Don't put a price on your health.

It has no dollar value.

The paramedics were there within 10 minutes.

They straightened my leg.

Bone ground against bone.
And my holler must have split every fine element in the sky.

They stuck an IV in my arm.
Put me on a stretcher and placed me in the ambulance.
I had ridden in ambulances before.
Seen dying patients.
Administered CPR.
And now I was in the ambulance.
These people were placing oxygen on me.
They were sticking me with those sharp needles.
I was taken to a hospital.
And was stuck in the Emergency Room for four hours.
Roles were reversed.
I was no longer in command.
I was the patient.
I was the one with an illness.
I was to wait in the ER.
I was to get pocked.
I was the one who received the x-ray.
Which by the way showed a fracture of the right femur (thigh).
And that's when the Orthopedic Surgeon came in the room, telling
me the news, as well as giving his opinion that a malignancy is the
most likely cause of the pathological fracture.
What was I to do?
Where was I to go?
How could I change my plight?
When would I find out?
Who was to help?
No way out of this one.
The bone was fractured.
I was to have surgery in a couple of days.
They would get the biopsy then.
I finally got out of the ER.
Only to find out that the surgeon wanted to hang my right leg in
traction so that the broken bones would align correctly prior to the
surgery.

Two holes were drilled through the right tibia (leg) and a metal rod was jammed into it so my leg could be suspended in the air, bent 90 degrees at the knee joint, with ten pounds of weight dangling and pulling my leg. A special contraption suspended by metal rails hung above my bed and made me feel as if I belonged in a circus show. Pain beyond belief.

And dignity?

You lose it.

Privacy?

Forget it.

It had never entered my mind that something like this could happen to me.

Something could actually change my plans.

Or even change my life.

I had my surgery.

Endured the six-day fiasco in the hospital.

Got news of my biopsy report.

And left.

I felt the humiliation that patients face when a gown is placed on them with the back open.

I felt the pain that patients feel when they become pincushions at four o'clock in the morning, just when they were getting some rest.

I felt the frustration of hitting the call button and having the nurse show up 30 minutes later.

I felt the anxiety of a much awaited biopsy report.

I had the nausea.

I had the sleepless nights.

I had the long awaited doctor visits that lasted *less* than one minute.

And I had that awful hospital food.

I was walking with crutches after the surgery.

A rod now resided in the marrow of my right femur.

Screws and pins safeguarded the rod in place.

Since I couldn't finish my Ob-Gyn rotation, my entire schedule for the third and fourth year medical school changed.

I would spend four weeks recouping at home.

And then return to medical school.

The biopsy report was negative.

And I returned home a different man.

-57-

ER Tour

Visit any Emergency Room.
You will soon find that tragedy may befall anyone.
It can affect the drunk as well as the sober.
It can affect the guilty as well as the innocent.
It can affect the adult as well as the child.
It can affect the known as well as the unknown.
It can affect the strong as well as the weak.
It can affect the visitor as well as the hometown resident.
It can affect the homeless as well as the homeowner.
It can affect the rich as well as the poor.
It can affect the employed as well as the unemployed.
No one seems to be exempt.
No one seems to have an escape.
No one seems to have the upper hand.
It is what people do with tragedy that ultimately matters.
I have seen people wither under tragic circumstances.
I have seen people's character show like never before.
I have seen some get bitter.
I have seen some get angry and blame everyone but themselves.
I have seen some pray.
I have seen some depressed.
I have seen some give up.
I have seen some fight to the last minute.
I have seen some overcome.
And I have seen some get stronger.

When one is faced with a certain circumstance, a choice is made.
Choices are made every day.
They are made on the freeways.
They are made at work.
They are made at home.
They are made at play.
How we choose to react is not in the hands of another person, some illness, or our circumstances.
How we choose to respond is entirely dependent on us.
And how we act defines our character.

-58-

Good from Bad

People change.

Plans change.

Possibilities at times are lost.

Promises at times are not kept.

Betrayal of a friend that is least expected can sink your heart.

Pain is inevitable in life.

Pound by pound your body will unfortunately take a beating.

We cannot afford to be like the twigs of a tree encrusted with ice that refuse to bow gracefully to their burden. If they resist bending, they will break. The trees in the evergreen forests of Canada endure the sleet and ice because they know how to bend. They bow down their branches and co-operate with the inevitable.

If we fight the inevitable, we will lose.

My Ob-Gyn rotation was over for the season.

I had to accept it.

I had to accept the fact that my leg was broken.

That I needed to rest.

That I needed to recover.

It would have done me no good to sit and complain about the fact that I lost time.

So I made changes in my schedule.

I bit the bullet and postponed my vacations.

And shifted rotations around.

Come what may, I wanted to graduate on time.

What has happened, has happened.

What is to be, will be.

I'm not sure why bad things happen to people.

I'm not sure why some have a full set of strings while others are forced to play on one string.

I suppose at times we deserve it.

I suppose at times we don't.

When faced with the inevitable, accept facts and move on.

And if you can, change, and overcome your circumstance.

I also believe that good things can come out of the bad.

That character is made in the fiery furnace.

I returned to school after four weeks.

With crutches.

And managed to complete my third year rotations.

Fourth year came by quickly.

I finished the incomplete Ob-Gyn rotation in my fourth year and moved on.

I was previously scheduled to complete my Internal Medicine (IM) rotation in the County Hospital. But with my broken femur and the schedule changes, I ended up rotating in a private hospital, Huntington Memorial Hospital (HMH) in Pasadena. This hospital changed my career choice. This new plan changed the course of my destiny.

I had shunned IM as a career choice because of the horrible experience in my first rotation in that field. Rotating in the private hospital gave me a different perspective. I changed my plans, and chose the Internal Medicine Residency Program at HMH. Over 660 people vied for six spots. And one of the six spots was mine.

It is true that bad things can happen.

It is up to us to absorb the blows.

And rise above our circumstances.

In my case, it is not a one-man effort.

In my life, it is a host of people investing their lives in mine to make my dreams come true.

-59-

TKO the Tech

I was complaining to the radiology department's supervisor regarding one of his workers.

I was extremely agitated.

An hour before, I was on the line with a radiology technician.

I was asking for a chest x-ray that was ordered two hours ago.

I said my patient needs the x-ray because I need to see the placement of a central line.

Amongst other statements, the tech replied, "Well, common sense would dictate that if you put the line in right, you could use it."

A sordid arrogance enveloped every word that sprang from his filthy mouth.

His cavalier attitude and demeaning tone offended me.

And my gut reaction was to knock him out.

In the same hospital, tragedy had stuck its ugly face through the corridors.

A young man—a distinguished physician—was battling cancer.

Cancer that had no cure.

No answers.

No life.

A diagnosis that came as a shock.

To the physician.

His family.

The hospital.

And the community.

After I came home, I thought about the physician and his family, and for a small moment felt their sorrow.

I whispered a prayer for him and his family.

In that moment, the radiology technician's voice spun its nasty web in the core of my memory.

Anger began to flare in my heart.
I was on my way to make this a federal case.
This was like a Supreme Court thing for my offended ego.
And then I froze.
Froze and thought about what I was doing.
Who cares if a tech told me I have no common sense?
Who cares if he was rude?
Who cares if he was entirely unprofessional?
Who cares if my ego got a bit crushed?
For that matter, who cares if someone cuts in front of me on the freeway?
Who cares if my name isn't mentioned on a program?
Who cares if the committee didn't like my suggestion?
Who cares if someone is served before I am?
Who cares?
And what does that have to do with the real stuff?
When it comes to the real stuff, the insignificant details don't and shouldn't matter.
With the real stuff, life is precious.
With the real stuff, family is priceless.
With the real stuff, friends are invaluable.
It takes me a while to get a point through my dense head.
And I'm just now beginning to understand.
That I need to get over the small things.
Cross over and feel the real zone.
Get myself settled in.
Live large.
Get my priorities in order.
And concentrate on the real stuff!

-60-

Living Beyond Your Case

Sitting through Chemistry
I did not understand
Sitting through Physics
Was a big time pain
Sitting through Organic Chemistry
Almost killed me
Sitting through Biology
Was mucho memory

Taking down notes
Word by word
Trying to learn
Everything I heard
Racing to class
Racing to soar
Racing to excel
Racing for more

Test after test
Day after day
Paper after paper
Without delay
You realize it's funny
That I forgot
What were once details
And now are not

Life goes on
No matter what you do
No matter who you are
No matter who knows who
No matter where you've been
No matter where you'll be
No matter what you want
No matter what you see

Live beyond
Beyond the stress
Beyond the grades
Beyond the tests
Beyond the competition
Beyond the race
Beyond the sweat
Beyond your case

Live by the truth
Live by the giving
Live by example
Live by loving
Live by peace
Live by sharing
Live by hope
And live by caring.
            —Dr. Rap

Take 5 with Dr. Rap

A man was looking for the special pet.

So he went to the pet store and asked the owner.

The owner told him that he had the perfect solution for him.

"Let me sell you this parrot… he'll talk forever… and will keep you company!"

So he sold him the parrot with a big cage.

The happy parrot owner went home with his new pet.

He tried everything, but couldn't get the parrot to talk.

One week later, he returned to the store and complained about the silent parrot.

"He doesn't say a word! He just sits there and stares as if I'm not there."

"Well, did you get him a mirror?"

"No."

"Well you see, your parrot needs a mirror! Once he sees himself… the mirror will prompt him to talk!"

The pet owner bought the most expensive mirror and went home excited.

A week passed.

No word from the parrot.

So he marched right back to the store and once again complained about the silent parrot.

"He sees himself in the mirror, but doesn't talk! What kind of bird did you sell me?"

"Did you get your bird a ladder?"

"A ladder?"

"Yes, a ladder! Your parrot can walk up and down the ladder, look at himself in the mirror and talk!"

The pet owner bought the fanciest ladder and once again went home with great hopes.

Another week passed.

No words.

The pet owner once again headed towards the store.

This time he was a bit agitated.

"Listen, your bird is dumb… he won't and probably can't speak!"

"I know what you're missing."

"What… what is it now?"

"A horn."

"A horn?"

"Yes! Place this horn in the cage. Once your bird hears the sound of a
 honk, it will entice him to speak."
"OK… I'll get the horn."
The custom-made horn was placed in the cage.
One more week of trials.
No words from the parrot.
The pet owner found himself in the store once again.
"What can we do to get this bird to talk?"
"I've got the solution for you. This will do the trick, I'm sure!"
"What… just tell me what!"
"Well, you need a swing. You can place this lovely swing in his big
 cage. He can swing, walk up and down the ladder, honk the horn,
 look at himself in the mirror, and then talk… guaranteed!"
This very special swing was purchased and brought home.
A week passed and the angry pet owner stormed back to the store.
"What's wrong?" the storeowner asked. "Is your bird OK?"
"He died!"
"He died?"
"Yes, he died!"
"Well, did he say anything before he died?"
"Yes he did."
"What… what did he say?"
"He asked, 'Don't they sell any food at that stupid store?'"

May sound crazy, but this is like real life.
We got the mirrors.
We got the ladders.
We got the horns.
The whistles.
The swings.
The works.
We go all out to pad ourselves.
But what of the essentials?
The real stuff?
The stuff that counts?
"Don't they sell any food at that stupid store of ours?"

144

Section VI

Passion

It is not the critic who counts
Not the man who points out how the strong man stumbled
Or where the doer of deeds could have done them better—
The credit belongs to the man who is actually in the arena
Whose face is marred by dust and sweat and blood
Who strives valiantly
Who errs and comes short again and again—
Because there is no effort without error and shortcoming—
Who does actually try to do the deed
Who knows the great enthusiasm
The great devotion
And spends himself in a worthy cause
Who at the worst, if he fails
At least fails while daring greatly.
Far better it is to dare mighty things
To win glorious triumphs
Even though checkered by failure and misunderstanding
Then to rank with those poor spirits
Who neither enjoy nor suffer much
Because they live in the grey twilight
That knows neither victory nor defeat.

—Theodore Roosevelt
26th President of the United States

-61-

Tad & Big Mac

The 1998 Major League baseball season was extreme!
St. Louis' Mark McGwire became an American hero, breaking the
home-run barrier by hitting 70 home runs.
And Chicago's Sammy Sosa was close behind.
A little kid named Tad was at a St. Louis home game watching
McGwire (BIG Mac) do his thing.
In Tad's hands was a small sign.
Small sign.
Small letters.
Huge message.
Tad was not only there to witness the BIG Mac drive.
In his mind and heart, he had a dream.
His sign read, "Field of Dreams... Maris... BIG Mac... Sosa... and ME
(Tad)."
With the baseball legends stands Tad.
Though 70 may no longer be the mark, there will be a time when
a baseball player will step up to bat and shatter the record.
The crazed fans will jolt to their feet, applaud, and scream in
mad joy.
The hearts of America will sing.
Kids will dream of the day when they too will play in the majors.
And Tad...
Tad will round the bases.
Heading for home plate.
Having just broken the homerun record.

-62-

Jerry & His Bullets

A friend e-mailed me this story.
I think you'll like it...

Jerry was a kind of guy you love to hate. He was always in a good mood and always had something positive to say. When someone would ask him how he was doing, he would reply, "If I were any better, I would be twins!"

He was a unique manager because he had several waiters who had followed him around from restaurant to restaurant. The reason the waiters followed Jerry was because of his attitude. He was a natural motivator. If an employee were having a bad day, Jerry was there telling the employee how to look on the positive side of the situation.

Seeing this style really made me curious, so one day I went up to Jerry and asked him, "I don't get it! You can't be a positive person all of the time. How do you do it?"

Jerry replied, "Each morning I wake up and say to myself, 'Jerry, you have two choices today. You can choose to be in a good mood or you can choose to be in a bad mood.' I choose to be in a good mood. Each time something bad happens, I can choose to be a victim or I can choose to learn from it. I choose to learn from it. Every time someone comes to me complaining, I can choose to accept their complaining or I can point out the positive side of life. I choose the positive side of life."

"Yeah, right, it's not that easy," I protested.

"Yes, it is," Jerry said. "Life is all about choices. When you cut away all the junk, every situation is a choice. You choose how you react to situations. You choose how people will affect your mood. You choose to be in a good mood or bad mood. The bottom line... it's your choice how you live life."

I reflected on what Jerry said. Soon thereafter, I left the restaurant industry to start my own business. We lost touch, but I often thought about him when I made a choice about life instead of reacting to it.

Several years later, I heard that Jerry did something you are never supposed to do in the restaurant business: he left the back door open one morning and was held up at gunpoint by three armed robbers. While trying to open the safe, his hand, shaking from nervousness, slipped off the combination. The robbers panicked and shot him. Luckily, Jerry was found relatively quickly and rushed to the local trauma center.

After 18 hours of surgery and weeks of intensive care, Jerry was released from the hospital with fragments of the bullets still in his body.

I saw Jerry about six months after the accident. When I asked him how he was, he replied, "If I were any better, I'd be twins. Wanna see my scars?"

I declined to see his wounds, but did ask him what had gone through his mind as the robbery took place. "The first thing that went through my mind was that I should have locked the back door," Jerry replied. "Then, as I lay on the floor, I remembered that I had two choices: I could choose to live, or I could choose to die. I chose to live."

"Weren't you scared? Did you lose consciousness?" I asked.

Jerry continued, "The paramedics were great. They kept telling me I was going to be fine. But when they wheeled me into the emergency room and I saw the expressions on the faces of the doctors and nurses, I got really scared. In their eyes, I read, 'He's a dead man.'

"I knew I needed to take action."

"What did you do?" I asked.

"Well, there was a big, burly nurse shouting questions at me," said Jerry. "She asked if I was allergic to anything. 'Yes,' I replied. The doctors and nurses stopped working as they waited for my reply. I took a deep breath and yelled, 'Bullets!' Over their laughter, I told them, 'I am choosing to live. Operate on me as if I am alive, not dead.'"

Jerry lived thanks to the skill of his doctors, but also because of his amazing attitude. I learned from him that every day we have the choice to live fully. Attitude, after all, is everything!

Attitude

Attitude can look at reality and rise above it.
Attitude can feel the shame and overcome it.
Attitude can sense the shortcomings and improve.
Attitude can carry you when you're too weak to move.
Attitude can bring your determination back.
Attitude can place you back on track.
Attitude is more precious than gold.
Attitude can bring you assets untold.
Attitude is more powerful than you and me.
Attitude can set your broken spirit free.
Attitude will destroy the invincible iron gate.
Attitude will set the tone for your fate.
Attitude will soften the crushing blow.
Attitude will strengthen your weary soul.
Attitude can cripple your deepest fears.
Attitude can dismantle your enemy's jeers.
Attitude is your source of hope.
Attitude is your lifeline to cope.
Attitude is relentless in helping you persevere.
Attitude is your ally when nothing seems clear.
Attitude revives the courage of your heart.
Attitude gives you strength from the start.
Attitude is a choice you make every day.
Attitude will save you tomorrow and today.
　　—Dr. Rap

-64-

Deaf Melodies

1800 and he realizes he is becoming deaf.
1802 and he is no longer in doubt that his malady is both
permanent and progressive.
1819 and his deafness becomes total.
He does not quit.
In fact, in one of his letters he writes, "I will seize fate by the throat."
1824 and his Ninth Symphony is finished and performed.
That Ninth Symphony was the last of his large-scale works.
Deafness would not and could not stop him.
He composed some of the most important works during the last ten
years of his life, when he was quite unable to hear.
No excuses.
No regrets.
No self pity.
No shutting down.
No giving up.
Beethoven kept striking keys to capture the imagination and hearts
of people who were and were to come.
Living passionately
And playing with soul…
On his last string.

-65-

From Schoolhouse to White House

How do you get from… no more than four months of formal education… to leading a country?
Determination.

How do you get from… a one-room country schoolhouse where the students range from age five to twenty-five… to writing the Second Inaugural Address, regarded by many as the noblest of all political documents?
Discipline.

How do you get from… listening to a teacher who probably had no more than an eighth-grade education… to etching out the Gettysburg Address?
Dream.

How do you get from… being one man, Abe Lincoln… to changing a whole world for the better?
Passion!

-66-

You Heard?

At times I question what I'm doing.
Why do I pursue rap music as Dr. Rap and speak in school assemblies, encouraging kids to stay in school and not mess with drugs?
Why do I visit prisons?
Why do I type this page?
Will it make a difference?
Shouldn't I instead invest all that money that goes to the studios and musicians in the stock market?
Shouldn't I instead give all that time to myself?
Am I just wasting my time?
At times I feel what I have done is worthless.
Why keep writing songs?
Why keep writing lyrics?
Why keep writing another page of this book?
At times I want to write the last line and call it quits.
Why go on when several music companies look at my work and say, "nice sound… but no sale… cuz there's no nasty edge?"
Why get up after I have fallen?
Why go on when I feel I have failed?
What is my motivation?
Is there anyone benefiting?
And then I get a letter.
From a kid saying thanks…
Saying he or she has memorized my songs…
Saying they won't mess with crack and cocaine…

Saying they will stay in school and study hard…
Saying they will respect themselves and their bodies by
not smoking…
Saying they will respect others.
And so I go on.
I write.
I rap.
I heal.
Because this is my feeble attempt to invest in the lives of children.
Because reaching one child may make a difference in a home…
In a community…
In a country…
And in *your* world.
Peace out.

-67-

Captains & Battleships

A battleship was on maneuver in severe weather for several days. One evening as night engulfed the foggy sea, the captain stayed on the bridge to decide his course.

The lookout on the wing of the bridge reported a light bearing on the starboard bow.

The captain asked, "Is it steady or moving astern?"

The lookout replied, "Steady, Captain."

This meant only one thing: both were on a collision course.

The captain called to the signalman, "Signal that ship to change its course 20 degrees to the north."

Back came this signal: "Change your course 20 degrees to the south."

The captain said, "I am a captain. Change your course 20 degrees to the north."

The reply came back, "I am a Seaman, Second Class. Change your course 20 degrees south immediately."

By this time the captain was furious. He exclaimed, "I am a battleship. Change your course 20 degrees north or suffer the consequences."

Back came the message, "Captain, I am a lighthouse. Change your course 20 degrees south... or face your final collision."

In your passion, don't fight with the inevitable.

-68-

Check Point

If we want to conquer
    We should also know how to serve.

If we want to have
    We should also know how to give.

If we want to win
    We should also know how to lose.

If we want to fly
    We should also know how to fall.

If we want to succeed
    We should also know how to fail.

If we want to be heard
    We should also know how to stay silent.

If we want to criticize
    We should also know how to take criticism.

If we want all the glory
    We should also know a little about humility.

If we want to be first
    We should also know how to be last.

If we want to be perfect
    We should also know that we're just human.

Review your life often, and make it worth living.
    —Dr. Rap

By Permission of Johnny Hart and Creators Syndicate, Inc.

-69-

Blood Tinged Soil

History tells us of a people who were robbed.
A meek people who were beaten senselessly.
Innocent men who were imprisoned unjustly.
Pregnant women who had their wombs slashed open brutally.
Unborn children who were stripped out of their mother's wombs
without mercy, and buried in the sand.
Fathers who witnessed the appalling crimes.
Mothers who felt the eternal pain.
Children who lost their loving bonds.
Thousands of men, women and children who were forced to walk
in the desert, whipped to death if they could not keep up with
the pace.
They were not given water or bread.
But they did taste the horrible stench of hatred.
They experienced the indescribable sting of jealousy.
And they died clinging to their God, who had for some unexplained
reason, allowed these atrocities to continue.
Swords were mostly used to kill because it was thought that a bullet
was too expensive to use on these people.
Barbaric and ruthless, the enemy raped the women and children.
The young ladies were literally stolen from their land and forced to
change their ethnicity and religion.
Thousands were forced into boats and then abandoned and
drowned.
Men were forced to sit on sharpened and gut stripping poles.
Heads were stacked in pyramids after "decapitation sessions."
1.5 million people were ruthlessly massacred.
Half of a nation was wiped out.

Till this day the nation that carried out the massacre, the rapes and the burials denies that these crimes took place!

That was in 1915.

When there was no media hype.

When the Turkish people seemed to get away with one of the cruelest acts recorded in history.

In fact Adolf Hitler wrote this on August 22, 1939: "I have given orders to my Death Units to exterminate without mercy or pity men, women, and children belonging to the Polish-speaking race. It is only in this manner that we can acquire the vital territory which we need. After all, who remembers today the extermination of the Armenians?"

Today, the Turkish government invests millions of dollars to cover up their shame.

They deny that the Armenian genocide ever happened, and have met with great success in doing so, for you will not find this story in many world history books.

Even Peter Jennings, the ABC World News anchorman was grossly negligent by omitting this significant event in his book, *The Century*. Despite irrefutable documentation, to this day the Turks adamantly swear that they never massacred the Armenian people.

The Armenians are my people.

They were living targets of bigotry, hatred and murder.

In the name of religion, they were killed.

And as I watched the news in 1998 and saw death being photographed in Kosovo some 83 years after the Armenian Massacre, I was saddened.

To think that there was an innocent child in Kosovo who died of hunger, under the reign of hatred.

Or for that matter, to think that black men and women were once lynched as a form of entertainment in our great country.

To think that at anytime anywhere an innocent soul could be persecuted in the name of prejudice.

To think that man could be so cruel as to carry out his hatred and then deny it.

To kill and have a clear conscience.
To injure and then to justify it.
To degrade and then laugh at the victim.
To bask in victory, knowing he has killed someone who was different.
Someone whose ethnicity threatens his world.
Unless you missed it, this and other violent behavior are not acts of
war, nor are they religious wars as the media proclaims.
Today, as you watch the Middle East in crisis, don't be fooled into
thinking that this is a "religious" thing...
It is a matter of hatred.
Hatred that's jealously harbored within one's soul.
It is man's inhumanity to man.

Though I commemorate the Armenian Massacre yearly, I do not
harbor bitterness toward the Turkish people.
Though I remember my grandfather showing me the gunshot
wound he acquired from the Turkish soldier while escaping his land,
I refuse to allow bitterness and hatred to paralyze me.
Bitterness enslaves.
Hatred kills.
It is too late to save the Armenian children buried in the blood tinged
soil.
But hatred is not the answer.

I will write to my congressman.
I will put the pressure on.
I will urge him to pass the resolution to proclaim to the world that
the Armenian genocide did truly take place.

But I will not hate.
Because hatred ends up killing me.

The few years that we have under the sun, we should strive not to
only take care of ourselves, but our neighbors around us.
To live with passion.
And to passionately love and protect each other... despite our
differences.

-70-

On Hatred, Jealousy & Love

Hatred.
It gnaws.
Tears.
Destroys.
Corrupts.
Blinds.
Kills.
And maims the soul.

Jealousy.
It breaks.
Harms.
Cheats.
Condemns.
Ruins.
Separates.
And shatters the heart.

Love.
It pardons.
Forgives.
Accepts.
Encourages.
Uplifts.
Embraces.
And sees no color.

Walk on the face of the earth.
Touch the hearts of people.
Invest in their lives.
Make a positive and eternal difference.
Bring joy to people's souls.
And rock your planet by choosing to love!
      —Dr. Rap

-71-

Giving with Passion

There was a charity fund.
One man donated $250,000.
Another gave $100.
Who gave more?
Whose money makes the difference?
There is no rocket science involved in this.
The man who donated the $250,000 gave more.
But consider this.
The man gave of his wealth with pride.
The other, a widow, gave her last penny with passion.
Setting all materialism aside, who gave more?

In this plastic world, you and I should strive to be known for our passion, generosity, humility and sincerity.

-72-

Open-Heart

Mr. D. ended up in the hospital with his second heart attack.
Fourteen years earlier, at the age of 40, he had an open-heart surgery for coronary artery disease.
And now, at the young age of 54, he underwent an attempted angioplasty[1] of a grafted vessel to his heart with unsuccessful results.
A balloon pump[2] was used to prevent him from decompensating.[3]
His cardiac profile fascinated me.
He was never a smoker.
Didn't have high blood pressure.
No signs of diabetes.
No cholesterol problems.
And no family history suggestive of premature coronary artery disease.
And had a bypass at a very early age.
Since I was on call the night of his procedure, I wanted to make sure he was tucked in well.
After speaking with him for a while, I asked him, "Mr. D., you don't have any risk factors for heart disease… why do you think you're struggling with this disease so much?"
"Anguish," he said, and caught me a little off guard.
Stress.
Grief.
Loss.
Loneliness.
Depression.
Anger.
Bitterness.

---

[1] *angioplasty:* opening an artery with a special balloon.
[2] *balloon pump:* instrument used to stabilize a patient with low blood pressure.
[3] *decompensating:* crashing; heart rate and blood pressure becoming unstable.

I had heard of these.

But never had I heard of a patient attribute his disease to anguish.

A deep.

Gnawing.

Indescribable.

Incessant.

Pain.

Mr. D.'s wife, whom he met at the age of 15, had suffered greatly from degeneration of her knee joints and had become wheelchair bound. She had also been diagnosed with breast cancer.

Mr. D.'s passion was his wife.

"I'll get back on my feet, doctor. I've got to see that she's well."

He cared for her.

Loved her.

And dedicated his life to uphold her.

I admired him for his strength.

I praised him for his courage.

And I encouraged him to fight on.

As I left the room, I was a bit depressed.

Why do bad things happen to sweet people?

I don't know.

Though I felt part of his pain, I couldn't even come close to understanding it.

I also left the room feeling challenged.

Mr. D. had more character and passion than I had witnessed in myself.

Anguish had put him on his back.

But passion would raise him to his feet.

Take 5 with Dr. Rap

In 1894, the rhetoric teacher at Harrow in England wrote on the sixteen year old's report card, "a conspicuous lack of success." The sixteen-year-old was Winston Churchill.

In 1902, the poetry editor of the Atlantic Monthly returned a sheaf of poems to a twenty-eight-year-old poet with this curt note: "Our magazine has no room for your vigorous verse." The poet was Robert Frost.

In 1905, the University of Bern turned down a Ph.D. dissertation as being irrelevant and fanciful. The young physics student who wrote the dissertation was Albert Einstein.

After the rejection, comes passion.
Passion will keep your eyes on the goal.
Passion will pick you up from the floor.
Passion will revive your soul to soar.
Passion will help you come back for more.

Section VII

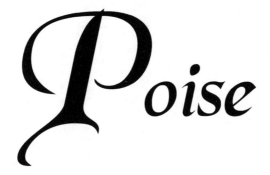

*A diamond is a chunk of coal
that performed well under pressure.*

—Author unknown

-73-

Essential Elements

The formula to help you reach your dreams does NOT exist.
There isn't a set way.
No matter what people say.
But there are elements.
That are essential.
Keep 'em close to your heart...
Hope.
Desire.
Will.
Perseverance.
Hard work.
Support.
Sacrifice.
Discipline.
Failure.
Enthusiasm.
Devotion.
Diligence.
Prayer.
Motivation.
Imagination.
Guidance.
Instructions.
Skill.
Knowledge.
Experience.
Humility.
Humility.
And more humility.

Planning.
Giving.
Sharing.
Improving.
Preparing.
Resting.
Relaxing.
Enjoying.
Learning.
Teaching.
Producing.
And don't forget...
Timing.
　　　　　—Dr. Rap

-74-

Extending Grace

A parable tells of a man who owed a great sum of money to
the king.

He was unable to make the payments and was brought before
the king.

He begged and asked the king for deliverance, mercy and
forgiveness.

The king was moved by the man's sincerity, and not only showed
mercy, but extended his grace and cancelled all the debts the
man owed him.

The man was shocked.

He left rejoicing.

A happy man.

A free man.

He had faced the possibility of losing his family and home.

He had faced the possibility of losing his freedom.

He had faced the possibility of losing his life.

But a merciful king erased his slate.

The man went home.

And called all the people who owed him money.

One by one.

One on one.

Speaking sternly.

He asked each what they owed him.

He asked each when the payments were due.

He did not ask them when they would be able to meet the
payments.

Nor did he care about their circumstances.

No matter what the people's plea.

He ignored the grace that was extended to him just hours before.

One by one, he demanded.

All of his debtors were unable to pay.
One by one, he threatened.
All begged for mercy.
One by one, he dragged to court.
All begged for him to extend the deadline.
One by one, he publicly scorned.
All begged on their knees.
But the arrogant, hardened and ungrateful man would not listen.
One by one, he threw in jail.
It wasn't long until the king heard of these rulings.
And called the man to his palace.
"Are you the man who could not pay his debts?"
"Yes sir, I am he."
"Are you the man that I forgave?"
"Yes sir I am."
"Are you the same one who has thrown innocent men into jail for
   small debts... debts that are minuscule compared to yours?"
The man bowed his head in fear.
"You are a shrewd man. A man who was forgiven... but a man who
   refuses to forgive... what have you to say to these charges?"
"Forgive me sir, but I... "
"Silence! You will be thrown in jail and will not be released until you
   pay back every cent you owe me. Now be gone from my sight."

To whom grace is extended, grace is expected.
To whom forgiveness is given, forgiveness is anticipated.
All of life is not for us.
All of life is not for gain.
All of life is not for building our own kingdom.
It is to serve others.
It is to forgive.
It is to love.
It is to show mercy.
It is to give.
The man in the parable lacked character by not extending the grace
that was given to him.
It is better to forgive than take vengeance.
It is better to show compassion than anger.
Where do you stand?
Where do I stand?
And are we willing to change?

174

-75-

Blue Codes with New White Coats

Internship year was more than a trip.
Fresh out of medical school.
I had passed two grueling national boards.
And was ready for the big leagues (with my first long white coat).
First time on call.
Freak time.
And I was scared!
I mean, I'm there!
And the patients... they're real!
And I'm taking care of them.
I grasped my "On Call" book and kept it chained to me.
What if... someone dies... is bleeding... can't breathe...
What if ... I have to intubate[1] someone... use the shock paddles...
What if ... I don't get to sleep...
What if ... I can't handle this...
"What ifs" cluttered my head, dancing to the beat of intimidation
  and fear.
The thoughts raced in my mind.
Wait.
I had four years of training.
I had back up.
I had worked hard.
Just then, my pager went off.
Not the normal pager ring.
The funny ring when there is a code.
"Code Blue... "
"Oh my God... this is real... the real thing... someone is dying..."

---

[1] *intubate:* insert a tube into the mouth and connect it to a ventilator (breathing machine) to
help someone breathe.

"Run Sam, run."

"Oh God help me. OK. Remember, Sam, just be calm. Breathe. Don't forget to breathe!"

I made it to the code.

The attending (veteran doctor) was looking at the electrocardiogram (EKG).

When I got there, he must have known I was a rookie.

He had never seen me before.

In fact, I had never seen him.

I looked at the EKG and mumbled a few words.

He looked at me and said, "It's OK, I think I've got everything under control… you don't have to stay."

I don't think I had interpreted the EKG correctly.

I don't think the attending was much impressed by my arrival.

I don't think he was seeking my help at that point.

That was my first code blue.

I went back to my other duties, mainly disappointed in myself.

Criticizing myself for not making a better first impression.

As I write this, I recall my last code blue as a senior resident, three years later.

Ironically, my last code as a resident took place in the same ward… with the same attending.

Funny how quickly three years past by.

Three national boards were successfully completed.

Skills were acquired.

Sleepless nights were spent roaming the hospital caring for the dying.

Thousands of orders were written.

Thousands of laboratory tests had been ordered.

And my "On Call" book collected dust on the shelf.
When I arrived at the code, the attending saw me walk into the room.
And he graciously allowed me to run the code.
Not as a rookie.
But as a senior resident.
Interpret those EKGs.
Push the Medications.
Get the IV access.
Intubate the patient.
Set the tone.
Set the pace.
Make the critical decisions.
And save the patient.
I don't think the attending remembers our first code together.
That's in the past.
And it's long forgotten.
What you and I do with our future is in our hands today.

-76-

Top 10

Dr. Rap's top ten list of a successful person:

10) One who has what he has but is not had by it.
 9) One who celebrates the gift of life before tragedy strikes.
 8) One who is able to give and receive love.
 7) One who displays character with words, deeds, attitude and life.
 6) One who continues to smile in his heart despite the betrayals.
 5) One who admits he's wrong and makes amends.
 4) One who has earned the respect and trust of children.
 3) One who helps the helpless and befriends the friendless.
 2) One who loves people and uses things, instead of using people and loving things.
 1) One who is ever achieving, creating and progressing, yet is content.

-77-

Be Still My Heart

Residency past and Cardiology, the study of the heart, became my passion.

Interviews went smoothly and I took one of the 45 spots offered in the state of California.

In my very first month of fellowship, I was thrown into the lion's den… into the cardiac catheterization room.

I remember my first angiogram case as a Cardiology fellow.

Scrubbing my hands with the blistering hot water.

And as the water dripped down my arm and made its escape to the ground, I marveled at the fact that 14 years of training had brought me to the Coliseum of Cardiology.

The anxious patient lay on the table.

The screens and monitors were set in place.

The confident technician meticulously set the table as if he were preparing for a war.

Masked and gowned, I moved to the right side of the patient.

The attending cardiologist stood beside me and seemed almost bored by the events, having done this for over 15 years.

I tracked each movement, every detail, and every word.

The heart monitor flashed the patient's living rhythm.

His heartbeat was regular, steady and in synch.

In the center arena of Cardiology, I felt my heart frantically tug and jab against my rib cage, beating faster than the patient's.

I looked over, and in a calm voice, asked the patient how he was doing.

"Oh fine, doctor."

"Great," I said, "We're about to begin."

"By the way doc... "

"Yes."

"How many of these have you done?"

Silence.

Complete silence.

The chatter in this arena came to an abrupt halt.

I looked over to the monitor, and felt paralyzed.

The patient's heart rate was still normal and in rhythm.

I felt the beads of sweat burrow through the pores of my forehead, as if each drop were screaming in horror, begging for refuge and desperately searching for shelter.

I began to hear my heartbeat churn in the chambers of my ears.

What was I to say to the patient?

If I say, "this is my first case," the patient would panic.

If I say, "many cases," I'd be lying.

If I don't say anything, the patient will ask again.

No one said a word as that one eternal second pinned me down to the mat.

The monotony of the case was shattered for the cath-lab team as they stared at me, intrigued, waiting to analyze every word that was to be uttered from the rookie's lips.

What would I say?

Where could I turn for help?

No one spoke.
No one offered to rescue.
And words started dripping from my lips, "Well sir, I've been a doctor for over three years now."
"OK doc."
And that was it.
I had seen case after case.
Observed.
Read.
Planned.
Prepared.
Passed three national boards.
Earned my medical license.
Completed residency.
And persevered to get to this stage.
And just like everyone, I had to start from the beginning, with my very first case.
I endured the cath.
The patient came out smiling.
The number of cases multiplied.
And having now done over 700 cases midway through my senior year… I'll never have to do my first angiogram again!

-78-

On How to Live

I find many people are imprisoned.
They are bound to the past.
Discontented with the present.
And terrified about the future.
I find many people are trapped.
Angry with their parents.
Angry with their children.
Angry at their circumstances.
Angry at the world.
Nothing will make them content.
Nothing will satisfy.
Nothing will fulfill.
This is life in the rat race.
See if you can relate to the following types of people.

There are the extreme optimists.
They lack reality.
They ignore the truth.

There are the pessimists.
They lack joy.
To them, everything is wrong.

There are the suspicious.
They lack trust.
Their walls are resurrected and you can't cross.

There are the fatalists.
They lack hope.
"Why try anyway?" they ask.

There are the realists.
They assess the situation.
Accept the inevitable.
Hope for the future.
And pursue their mission.

If you're going to play life 101, know where you stand.
The only way to live life fully is to face it.
It's to deal with it.
It's to live realistically.
Live courageously.
Live enthusiastically.
And live wholeheartedly.

-79-

Your King

Long ago, a group of musicians lived in a faraway land.
They traveled from town to town singing and playing their music in hopes of making a decent living.
Times were hard, and people were unwilling to pay the concert fees, even though the group's fees were small.
One evening the group met to discuss their future.
"I see no reason for opening tonight," said one of the musicians. "It's snowing and no one will come out on a night like this."
Another said, "I agree! There was only a handful last night, and fewer will come tonight."
After the leader of the group listened to all the complaints, he said, "I know you are discouraged. I am too, but we have a responsibility to the folks that might come tonight. Let's go out there and do the best job that we are capable of doing. Those who come should not be punished for those who don't."
Heartened by his words the musicians gave their best performance ever.
After the show, the leader called all the members back stage.
In his hand was a note, handed to him by one of the audience members.
Slowly the man read the words that changed the destiny of the group.
"Thank you for your beautiful performance."
It was signed simply, "Your King."

When people are watching you, do your best.
When nobody is watching you, strive for excellence.

-80-

Pacemaker Frenzy

Words cannot describe how inadequate I felt when I had my first
pacemaker clinic as a first year Cardiology fellow.
There were at least three different machines that interrogate the
patients' pacemakers.
All different companies.
And they all program a pacer differently.
The technician began explaining how to interrogate and change a
pacemaker's parameters.
I listened and asked questions.
The patient looked a bit surprised.
There I was.
With a white coat.
With my name, and the word "Cardiology" on it.
I felt embarrassed asking the simple questions as the patient looked
at me in bewilderment. Wasn't I supposed to know all this? And if I
didn't, what was I doing in the room anyway? One of the attendings
(no white coat and no sports coat … just a badge backed by twenty
years of experience) walked in, greeted us, assessed the patient,
glanced at the computer, made some adjustments and made it look
simple. Way too simple. I could see the relief on the patient's face as
she regained her confidence that at least one of the doctors knew
what in the world he was doing.
Funny how I went from being a senior resident, confident in my skills
in Internal Medicine, to a rookie in Cardiology, overwhelmed by the
amount of skills I was to learn.
But there will come a time when I will be as skilled as my mentors.
There will come a time when I will walk in, see the patient, look at
the numbers on the pacemaker, and say, "Let's do this."
Bam, just like that.

There will come a time…
When what seems impossible is actually simple.
When what seems overwhelming is actually uncomplicated.
When what seems unconquerable is actually effortless.
When what seems insurmountable is actually routine.
The journey is not easy.
At times I am discouraged.
And feel like quitting.
At times I feel overwhelmed.
And feel like I'm inadequate.
At times I feel like that little boy trying to play football on
American soil.
But I am always hopeful.
And am always ready.
Ready to learn.
Ready to live humbly.
And ready to perform with excellence.

-81-

Would Have Never

I would have never
Moved to the U.S. of A.
If my parents did not work over 15 hours a day.

I would have never
Adapted to my new culture fully
If kind people did not adopt my family.

I would have never
Made it into medical school
If I quit when they called me a fool.

I would have never
Passed Microbiology
If it weren't for friends helping me.

I would have never
Come this far.
If I didn't dream, plan, and work hard.

I would have never
Made it through the days
If it weren't for God's undeserved grace.
   —Dr. Rap

-82-

Character Flaws

Does character really matter?
Can you and I lead a people and be morally corrupt?
Can you and I say one thing and do another?
Can you and I be involved in drugs and yet be role models?
Can you and I live a life of hypocrisy and become heroes to kids?
Can you and I afford to take the risk?
Can one's impressive credentials nullify his or her flaws of character?
Can one's spectacular skills blind the fact he or she can lie, cheat, steal,
hate, destroy, disregard the truth, and bask in self indulgence?
It happens every day.
We can be corrupt and lead at the same time.
We can say one thing and do another.
We can be heroes and yet be hypocrites.
But we shouldn't.
And it shouldn't be tolerated.
We should curb our appetites.
And we should set pace for the future generations.

"If we teach them racism, they will learn to hate.
We must encourage unity, 'cuz in us they place their faith.
If we teach them violence, they will learn to destroy
So we must place peace in the hearts of every girl and boy
If we teach them pornography, they will learn to be corrupt
So we must instill the truth in their hearts and minds
If we teach them deception, they will learn to mistreat
We must encourage compassion so they'll help their neighbor in need."
(Lyrics from Dr. Rap's *Cut to the Heart*, "Our Future").

Our examples will far outlive our accomplishments.
Character does matter.
Don't convince yourself otherwise!

-83-

Baby Girl Smile

Natalie is a two-year old baby girl.
And awaits her second open-heart surgery.
She does not talk.
But her smile sings a thousand songs of love and happiness.
Multiple congenital malformations have restrained her to a life on oxygen tubes. She has cataracts, no thymus, heart defects, and only one functional kidney. A gastric tube hangs from her belly, this being the lifeline to all of her nutrition.
She touches her daddy's hand to make sure he's there.
She looks at her mom to be reassured of her presence.
And she smiles.
My problems seem to vanish as I listen to her musical heart.
Her head dangles to one side because of her weak neck muscles.
Because I am just visiting in the Pediatric clinic for the week and only specialize in adult Cardiology, I am a bit surprised to see an open-heart incisional scar on a two year old.
Natalie will soon get her angiogram.
And then will face her second surgery.
Though she cannot verbalize her pain, she will face many problems in this life, and will cry many tears.
But for now, she has her wonderful parents who support her and love her.
And just like an angel, she smiles.
And it's that baby girl smile that reminds me...
Concentrate on the real stuff!

-84-

Contracting for Life

There are three significant days in your life.
The day you were born.
The day you find the purpose in your life.
And today.
My wish for you is that you grasp this day by the jugular, and live life with poise and passion.
To do so, you need some direction.
Make yourself a contract.
Sign it.
Then live by it…

As an example, I have set before you my own contract in this very short and fleeting life. By no means is it complete; it is just a part of me that I share with you:

The more I gain, the more I'll give.
The more I have, the more I'll share.
The more I know, the more I'll teach.
The more I succeed, the more I'll invest in the lives of others.
The more I achieve, the more I'll be gracious.

My mission is to heal.
With a smile.
With an encouraging word.
With a willing heart.

I vow to act justly.
To love mercy.
And to walk humbly.

I will use all the skills and gifts bestowed upon me by God to touch and mend the hearts of a broken generation and challenge them to live a life of excellence.

This is my mission.
This is my goal.
This is my life.

If you haven't yet done so, write your purpose down.
Let it come to life.
Let it resound with hope.
And let it change the course of your life.

My purpose:

Signature:

Date:

-85-

Impress Me

I am not impressed by
One's positions
One's possessions
One's records
One's degrees
One's might
One's ratings
One's accomplishments
One's appearance
One's arrogance
One's brilliance
One's curriculum vitae, or resume
One's speed
Or one's eloquence.

I am impressed by
One's humility
One's willingness to share
One's deep compassion
One's unwavering integrity
One's acts of justice
One's kind smile
One's warm welcome
One's sacrifices
One's gentle attitude
One's gracious manner
One's ability to forgive
One's enthusiasm
And one's honorable character.
   —Dr. Rap

-86-

On Living Humbly

Meekness said to arrogance, "After you."
Arrogance replied, "Get out of my face."
Arrogance stepped in front of meekness.
And fell.
Arrogance is disgusting.
Arrogance is a defense mechanism for wimps who are insecure about themselves.
Arrogance goes hand in hand with pride.
And pride leads to a major fall.

Forgiveness said to anger, "I forgive you for what you did to me."
Anger replied, "What do you mean, 'I forgive you.' I didn't do anything."
Anger turned its back on forgiveness.
And died within.
Harbored anger is harmful.
Anger is appropriate in certain circumstances.
But if unchecked it can become explosive.
And if it turns into bitterness, it churns the life out of your bones.

Charity said to stingy, "You can have all you need."
Stingy replied, "I deserve it; I'll take it all."
Stingy took but never gave.
And never had joy or peace in his heart.
Being stingy is a form of deprivation.
We deprive ourselves of giving.
We deprive ourselves of joy.
And we live in complete misery.

-87-

Money Can't Buy

Gifts you can't buy:
Satisfaction in your work.
Enjoyment of life.
Contentment in your heart.

"Money buys luxury, can't buy joy
If you're looking for the answer, it ain't in your toy
Money buys cars, can't buy honesty
Money buys favors, can't buy mercy
Money buys gold, can't buy beauty
Money buys flattery, can't buy sincerity
Money buys vacations, can't buy serenity
Money buys alarms, can't buy security

Money buys stocks, can't buy sleep
Listen up my homey, what I'm saying is deep
Money buys food, can't buy an appetite
Money buys glasses, can't buy your sight
Money buys clothes, can't buy you character
Money buys fame, can't buy you honor
Money buys land, can't buy creation
Money buys books, not imagination"
        (Lyrics from Dr. Rap's *Cut to the Heart*, "Money Can't Buy")

If our motive is money, we'll never have enough.
If little ain't enough, more won't satisfy.
And if more won't satisfy, we'll never be happy.

Make all you can.
Save all you can.
But remember, to give all you can.

By Permission of Johnny Hart and Creators Syndicate, Inc.

~88~

Life & Death

Have you ever been asked a question about your death?
Has anyone approached you.
And said.
"When you die, what do you think people will say about you?"
"When you die, what would you like people to say about you?"
That's not where I'm going with this chapter.
My question is not about the dead.
My concern isn't about the grave.
Cuz in the grave there ain't no strength.
Nor energy.
Nor life.
Nor wisdom.
Nor hope.
Nor dreams.
My question to you and me is this.
What do people say about us *now*?
What would you like people to say about you?
I'm not asking us to live for others.
Nor am I asking us to be suspicious of those around us.
But because we interact with people on a daily basis, it does matter.
It matters how we treat one another.
It matters whether we are rude or constantly irritable.
It matters if our tongue has a bitter edge.
It matters whether we help one another.
And it matters if our attitude reeks with complaints.
If we are to love, why wait for tomorrow?
If we are to help, why not help today?
If we are to encourage, why not uplift someone when it is in our power to do so?

In the grave, breath does not exist.
It don't matter then.
What matters is now.
There is a time for everything.

"There's a time to laugh and a time to weep.
A time to throw away and a time to keep.
A time to mourn and a time to dance.
A time to be exact and a time to take a chance.
A time to hold on, a time to let go.
A time to say yes and a time to say no.
A time to embrace and a time to refrain.
A time for sunshine, a time for rain."
        (Lyrics from Dr. Rap's *Licensed to Heal*, "Time Zone")

It's time.
Time to love.
Time to encourage.
Time to help.
And a time to make a difference in people's lives.
Today.

Unfortunately, we are a bit on the stubborn side.
We tend to learn through tragedies.
I have seen families who are geographically close but estranged in heart as they gather to visit their parents or spouses who are dying in our cardiac care unit. Some desperately scream at each other while others turn in vengeance to yell at the doctors and nurses. They are there to save mom or dad. They are there to mend the past. They are there to say they are sorry for what they had said or failed to say. And they are there to do it all in two to three hours. They scramble for words. Scramble for time. And search for a meaning in death.

What the families would give to have a meaningful conversation with their kids who were shot in Littleton, Colorado in 1999 by the Trench Coat Mafia.
What the parents would give to stop and take a day off to take a child to Disneyland before that child is diagnosed with Leukemia.
What a husband would give to send roses to his wife before she is diagnosed with breast cancer.
What you and I would give to say kind words to a loved one whom we lost in a tragic death.
How the tones of voices would change.
How little annoyances would be overlooked and forgiven.
How the important stuff like love would take center stage.

I hope you and I are not waiting for tragedy or death to wake us up.
Because by then.
When.
The coffin is shut.
And breath and body turn to naught.
Then.
It is too late.

-89-

Give it Up

What we can give away per day:
10 smiles.
 9 (times forever) acts of love.
 8 hugs.
 7 (times eternity) acts of forgiveness.
 6 encouraging words.
 5 minutes of our busy lives for someone else.
 4 acts of kindness.
 3 attempts at selflessness.
 2 kisses.
 1 small note of appreciation.

Ten more of my favorites:
 1) Choose to be happy.
 2) Learn from children.
 3) Hear the birds sing before you get to work.
 4) Love like you've never been betrayed.
 5) Floss your teeth.
 6) Sing like mad.
 7) Praise in public.
 8) Criticize in private.
 9) Don't be arrogant.
10) Choose to be creative.
        —Dr. Rap

-90-

Laughing Clowns

In the early 1800s in Manchester, England there lived a lonely man.
Depressed.
Dejected.
Distraught.
Dismayed.
He turned to alcohol.
Found no comfort.
He turned to friends.
Found no compassion.
He turned to money.
Found no happiness.
He turned to self.
And found no salvation.
So he went to a psychiatrist.
"I'm not feeling good, doc, I'm just not feeling good."
"What's on your mind... what's bothering you?"
"I feel so depressed... so down.
I want to smile, but I can't.
I want to sing, but I don't.
I want to laugh, but I cry.
A sense of doom envelopes me.
A sense of darkness shadows me.
A sense of loss haunts me.
I can't sleep.
I've lost my appetite.
Nothing is fun anymore."
"Tell me about your situation... have you lost a loved one... or a
job... what's depressing you?"
"I've lost nothing.
I have everything one would want.

A beautiful wife.
A beautiful child.
A wonderful job.
I just feel empty."
"How long have you felt this way?"
"Oh, I don't know... it's been a gradual thing."
"Is it getting worse?"
"I guess it's the same... I'm not sure... can you prescribe me
something?"
"Well, let me ask you this."
"Yes."
"Have you thought about harming or killing yourself?"
"I might... I just don't know."
"Do you have a plan... a means of harming yourself?"
"No... I just want to enjoy things once again!"
"So you don't want to harm yourself?"
"No... I just want to laugh from within."
"Have you gone out lately... spent some time with the family?"
"No."
"You know there is a circus in town?"
"Yes."
"It's the talk of the town. The adults love it... kids are going crazy.
Here, look, it's in the paper. They've got a picture of the clown,
Grimaldi. He's a smash hit. He had me almost rolling on the floor...
he's a crack up... the audience was going mad last night... why
don't you take your family? Why don't you break the routine a bit?
Enjoy... laugh... this clown will get you good... I know it! What do
you think?"
"This clown had you going huh, doc!"
"I know it's only for a few hours... but man... he's good."
"Doc."
"Yes."
"That clown... "
"Yes."
"That clown is me."

Sometimes things aren't as they seem.

Sometimes people aren't as they appear.

But everyone, no matter how established or confident, has some burden or problem.

One of man's deepest longings is to be encouraged, appreciated and loved.

Did you know that your simple smile could change someone's demeanor?

Your simple handshake can make someone feel welcome.

Your simple hug can lighten up someone's day.

Your simple words of encouragement can make a difference in one's goals and dreams.

Your simple card can dramatically impact one's attitude.

Don't underestimate the power of your kindness towards others, even if they *seem* as if they don't need it!

-91-

What's Up with That!

On the road to my goals, I had not tasted humility for a long time.
Years of training were completed.
Three national boards were successfully taken and my medical license acquired.
Next on the list was passing the Internal Medicine boards.
On November 14, 1998, three months after taking the boards, I received the results.
The years of learning.
The months of reading.
The two harsh days of taking the test.
Question after question.
Racing against time.
Struggling to make sense of ambiguous questions.
When I opened the letter.
I felt as if I received the ever-familiar letter of apology of the past.
The ones I used to get attempting to gain access to medical school.
The ones I thought I'd never see again.
The ones that start with, "We regret... "
It had been a while since I had read those words.
Getting into medical school was torture.
I had finished my residency in Internal Medicine and had just started my fellowship in Cardiology.
And on this exam, I missed the passing mark by four questions.
That's not much when you consider that there were 480 questions in the exam.
I asked, "Why... why me... why now?"
I felt that I would be tagged.
"Oh... he's the Cardiology fellow that failed his boards. The others passed... what's wrong with him?"

I felt inadequate.

I felt like quitting.

I felt undeserving of my position in Cardiology.

I felt that terrible tug of failure lurking in my heart.

With a certain amount of success, we tend to forget about our humble beginnings.

And feel like success will follow us all the days of our lives.

The bottom line is.

I failed that test.

But I didn't fail life.

Like that little boy playing football on American soil, I am still vulnerable.

And able to make mistakes.

Failing is a part my life.

It comes with the territory of living.

It comes with the package of success.

It can happen any time.

Even if I have my guard up.

Even if I am prepared for victory.

I am unable to control everything every time.

I have once again faced failure.

It has brought me low.

It has brought me down.

But it has not crushed me.

The result of the exam is like a single minor note in a piece played by an orchestra.

Judging from my past, a simple minor note adds incredible depth to the entire piece.

And along with the rejections from record labels.

Along with the rejections from publishers.

My recent failures seem to be multiplying.

These failures do not define my person.

They do not shape my compassion.

They do not dictate my future.

I'm not sure where you are in your life.
You may be enjoying success.
Or you may be lying in a hospital bed with an uncertain future.
You may be in a divorce trial.
You may have lost a child, a spouse or a parent.
Your closest friend may have dealt you one of life's most bitter pills, the one of betrayal.
You may have just been cut from the team.
You may be laid off.
A member of your family may be facing an illness or unthinkable charges.
You may be going through the darkest shadows of life, immersed in depression.
You may have failed the interview.
Or just barely missed the mark.
You may not have met your expectations.
Or the expectations of someone else.
You may be scared.
You may be lonely.
You may be down.
You may be feeling extremely tired.
Discouraged.
Defeated.
Or even apathetic.
And you too may be playing on your last string.

No matter what, I have learned that it's not worth fighting the inevitable.
It's not worth chasing the shadows of defeat.
I have learned that if I can change a situation, I will change it.
If I can improve it, I will improve it.
And if I must accept it, I will accept it.

If you are playing on your last string…
Play your heart out.
Play like you belong.
Play like you own the court.
Play hard.
Play strong.
And play with soul.
Reclaim your dream.
Redeem yourself.
Resolve your issues.
Rebuild your future.
If there is no wind, row.
If there is no string, hum.
And if you want to quit, don't.

As for me, I have decided to view life as a challenge, and not as a threat.
My greatest defeats have become my greatest victories.
I will hit the books once again.
I will write my songs to change lives.
I will write my books to inspire souls.
I will love life.
I will love people.
And I will practice medicine with great skill and undeniable compassion.
For I've got the essentials on my side.
I got purpose.
I got love.
And I got faith.

By the way.
You know by now that I'm not the best test taker.
But.
I passed the Internal Medicine boards the second time around.
And just in case you wondered…
I'll see you.
At the Grammy's!